U. C. L. A.
Students' Store
7407S
.89

S0-BRL-291

THE PRIVATE WORLD OF WILLIAM FAULKNER

By the same author

THE WINE OF GENIUS:
A LIFE OF MAURICE UTRILLO

The Private World of

WILLIAM FAULKNER

by Robert Coughlan

Illustrated

HARPER & BROTHERS, PUBLISHERS

New York

THE PRIVATE WORLD OF WILLIAM FAULKNER

Printed in the United States of America

FIRST EDITION

I-D

Library of Congress catalog card number: 54-8943

TO RUTH ANN EASTMAN

ACKNOWLEDGMENTS

Among the many sources consulted, the author owes a special debt to Robert Cantwell's preface to *The White Rose of Memphis* by Colonel William C. Falkner (Coley Taylor, 1953), to Ward L. Miner's *The World of William Faulkner* (Duke University Press, 1952), and to Frederick J. Hoffman and Olga W. Vickery, *Faulkner—Two Decades of Criticism* (Michigan State College Press, 1951).

Thanks are due also to Random House for permission to quote from several of William Faulkner's books, and especially to *Life* Magazine, in which some of this material first appeared.

CONTENTS

ILLUSTRATIONS

These illustrations will be found in a group following page 64.

THE PRIVATE WORLD OF WILLIAM FAULKNER

1

YOKNAPATAWPHA AND ITS "SOLE PROPRIETOR"

Jefferson, the county seat of Yoknapatawpha County, in northwest Mississippi, is a pretty town with an old brick courthouse, pillared and porticoed, on a big central square, and a number of big, white-pillared houses set in broad lawns, although some of the finest homes were lost when General A. J. Smith partially burnt the town in 1864. Jefferson has practically no manufacturing, but lives on, and in turn nourishes, the surrounding countryside, which is given over largely to cotton and lumbering. At the last official census (1946) the county, which takes in 2,400 square miles, had a population of 15,611. A passing stranger would find little to distinguish the town and the county from many such towns and counties in Mississippi or in all that area of the deep South. Nor is it likely that he would think the people different from others in that domain. If the stranger were a Southerner, he would feel very much at home there.

Given omniscience, however—the literary omniscience of a novelist, for instance—and suspended from a large gas bag so as to obtain a wide view of the countryside, the stranger would discover that the peaceful aspect of Jefferson and Yoknapatawpha County was an illusion. Indeed, except among the children and Negroes, and some hunters and old men and old women, he would have a hard time finding the quality of peace anywhere. Looking into the hearts and minds and studying the actions of most of the adult white population, the balloonist could not help but be appalled at what he saw.

Peering down on Frenchman's Bend, a hamlet in the southeast part of the county, he would find a man named Flem Snopes cheating and manipulating his neighbors until at last he controlled them all, marrying the daughter of his most important victim, swindling a farmer with a nonexistent buried treasure and driving him insane, and moving on to Jefferson with his tribe of decadent relatives to corrupt that town (1).* At this same hamlet years later (the omniscient aerialist can also telescope time as novelists do), he would see a college girl named Temple Drake fall into the hands of a gunman named Popeye, who rapes her in a macabre way and afterwards installs her in a Memphis house of

* For the meaning of the numbers in parentheses see footnote, p. 19.

prostitution and engages a friend to further violate her, whereupon she becomes a victim of passion; Popeye eventually is executed for a crime he did not commit and Temple's father takes her to Paris (2).

Drifting away from Frenchman's Bend, the aerialist would notice with interest the tribulations of the Bundren family: the death of Addie Bundren, a hill woman, the building of her coffin, and the long trip by wagon to the cemetery in Jefferson accompanied by her shiftless husband, her pregnant unmarried daughter, and her four sons. Her body putrifies and attracts vultures, is swept away in a flooded river but is recovered, nearly burns in a barn fire but is saved, and is buried at last. One son is led from the graveside to a lunatic asylum; another, the youngest, believes his mother is a fish. The father, having cheated another son of his horse, and his daughter of the money her lover had given her for an abortion, buys new false teeth and marries a woman from whom he had borrowed a shovel to dig his wife's grave. She has a phonograph, and the eldest boy thinks it will be nice to have music in the home (3).

Bearing north over the pine hills and eroded cotton land until he neared Jefferson, the aerialist would arrive over "Compson's Mile" and would be shocked to see the situation to which this once-great plantation and once-great family had fallen. There are the parents and their four children: the father is alcoholic, the mother neurasthenic, the daughter pregnant with a stranger's child, one son an idiot, another selfish and villainous, the third proud, romantic but weak. He would see this last-named boy, Quentin Compson, pretend that he had committed incest with his sister and finally commit suicide; the idiot brother castrated and sent to an institution; the sister marry, divorce, and give herself to a succession of lovers; the wicked brother hound his sister's illegitimate daughter and drive her away, sell the old plantation house, and use the proceeds to establish himself as a cotton broker and to acquire a mistress, a Memphis prostitute (4).

There is the sound of gunfire to the north. The aerialist swings in a favoring current and views a wild scene—horsemen galloping, Negroes stampeding toward a river, an old woman burying treasure, boys crouched in the bushes shooting at Yankee soldiers, the same old woman being shot, the same boys tracking her assassin, flaying him and nailing his skin to a barn door. But amidst all the tumult the overpowering figure of Colonel John Sartoris is seen in actions of amazing initiative and gallantry. He raises a regiment in Jefferson and gallops off to Manassas; demoted by his own men, who elect an upstart named Sutphen to his command, he returns to Jefferson, raises a new regiment and gallops off again, this time to serve with General Forrest's raiders. The war over, he disciplines the carpetbaggers, builds a railroad the length of the county and is shot dead by a scoundrel (5).

The Colonel's heirs live on in the shadow of his memory. His son becomes president of the bank in Jefferson and dies of heart failure due to the reckless driving of his great-grandson. The grandson is scarcely seen, living only long enough to marry and produce this great-grandson and his twin brother, both of whom are pilots in the First World War. The twin is killed in France; the other, obsessed with this event and blaming himself for it, afterward lives in spiritual torment, and at last kills himself testing an experimental airplane (6).

Off to the northwest there is a commotion in the forest: wild, naked Negroes heaving and sweating, felling trees, dragging huge logs, sawing them into boards, at last rearing a splendid house surrounded by a lovely park and sweeping fields. A big, grim-faced man gallops about on horseback: he is Sutphen, the same who (later) ousted Colonel Sartoris from the command of the regiment. He must build a dynasty, and this great house to shelter it; but his plans are doomed. He disowns his first son when he discovers that there is Negro blood in the mother's family. This son falls in love with Sutphen's daughter by a second marriage and is killed by his half-brother, who becomes a fugitive. Coming home years later, the half-brother dies in a fire that consumes the house. Sutphen meantime, ruined by the Civil War but still hoping for a son to whom he can pass his name and ambitions, seduces the granddaughter of a squatter and is killed by him (7).

In the far north there is the wilderness, and Indians can be seen in their villages. Then the Indians disappear, and white men and boys come and set up camps and hunt for game (especially, for one huge, crafty old bear), and then the wilderness itself disappears as the timber companies move in (8). The aerialist drifts south again and hovers over Jefferson, that deceptively quiet town. There Temple Drake can be seen, married now and working out the tortured sequel to her earlier mishaps (9). Here and there on the streets is a Compson or Sartoris or the friends of those families, an Edmonds, De Spain or McCaslin, but the town seems to be overrun with Snopeses. They are everywhere, even in the Sartoris bank. Odd and terrible things are happening. Joe Christmas, illegitimate and probably part Negro, is put in an orphanage, then adopted by a stern and righteous farmer and his wife. Joe beats the farmer and steals the wife's savings, has an affair with the spinster descendant of Yankees, kills her and is pursued around the county and captured. His own grandfather incites a mob to lynch him. But he escapes, only to be hunted down by a patriotic young man named Percy Grim, who shoots and mutilates him.

Meantime a girl named Lena Grove, pregnant by Christmas's partner in the bootlegging business, has journeyed on foot from Alabama to find him so he can claim the child. But he flees; and she goes back to Tennessee with her baby (10).

Here, too, is seen Lucas Beauchamp, an old Negro accused of murder and about to be lynched. But he is saved by the courage of a white boy, a Negro boy and an old maid (11). And here also, among many other scenes of horror and bravery, can be found an old woman who, fearing that her husband would leave her, has killed him and laid him on his bed and kept him thus until he became a mummy (12).*

The aerialist is, of course, imaginary, but so are Jefferson and Yoknapatawpha County. The town and county—it can be said with relief—are the literary inventions of William Faulkner, who is their "sole proprietor." And if they bear a resemblance in many details to Lafayette County, Mississippi, and its county seat

* Faulkner's books are extraordinarily discursive and complex, not "plotted" in the ordinary sense but seeming rather to have grown according to their own internal dynamics, resulting in many subplots and *cul de sacs.* However, in briefest outline, these are the stories told in (1) *The Hamlet,* (2) *Sanctuary,* (3) *As I Lay Dying,* (4) *The Sound and the Fury,* (5) *The Unvanquished,* (6) *Sartoris,* (7) *Absalom, Absalom!* (8) *The Bear,* (9) *Requiem for a Nun,* (10) *Light in August,* (11) *Intruder in the Dust,* and (12) his most famous short story, *A Rose for Emily.*

of Oxford, where Faulkner lives, it is still true (however one may feel about the events he makes happen there) that in inventing them he has achieved one of the most impressive feats of imagination in modern literature. His accomplishment was recognized most notably in 1950 when he received the Nobel Prize for literature, and he has been given many other honors, among them the rank of Officer in the French Legion of Honor.

Faulkner has accepted these testimonials laconically, with few signs of pleasure or even of interest. While speaking well of the Nobel Prize, it was only under great family and official pressure that he consented to travel to Sweden to receive it. He dislikes "literary" events, especially when they involve him as a principal, and "literary people," especially those who wish to discuss his books with him. Nor does he feel any warmth for his readers, whose opinions and, indeed, whose existence is a matter of indifference to him. He dislikes publicity or public notice, and any attempt to penetrate his privacy is met with an irascible and incendiary anger.

Yet it is no more possible for Faulkner to remain inconspicuous than it would be to build a wall around the Grand Canyon. His books—labyrinthine, grandiose, grotesque and beautiful—are no longer his but have become a part of the literary landscape of his country, like Melville's and Poe's. Because he has created them, he does not belong entirely to himself.

William Faulkner is a small, wiry man with closely cropped iron-gray hair; an upswept mustache of a darker color; a thin, high-bridged aquiline nose; heavy-lidded and deeply set brown eyes in which melancholy, calculation and humor variously are reflected; and a face tanned and webbed, especially near the eyes, with the creases and lines and tiny tracings of advancing middle age and the erosion of many days spent in the open in all weathers. He is entirely self-possessed, with a manner easy, courteous, speculative, and deadly. He is a quiet man; yet when he is at ease, with his short legs outstretched and a blackened pipe in his thin lips, and perhaps a drink at his elbow, he is like a somnolent cat who still in the wink of an eye could kill a mouse. Faulkner does not look or act like what he is. He acts like a farmer who had studied Plato and looks like a river gambler. In the way he looks there is something old-fashioned, even archaic.

Oxford, like Faulkner's imaginary town of Jefferson, lies in the northwest part of Mississippi and has a population of about 4,000. It is intensely and unmistakably a town of the deep South, not only in its appearance but in its smells, its manners and morals, the speech and proprieties of its citizens. Faulkner lives in one of its most beautiful houses, built circa 1840 by an Irish planter, Colonel Robert Shegog. It had fallen into terrible decay, but Faulkner gradually has restored it since he bought it in 1930 and now it is in good shape, although several rooms still remain to be done over. The house sits at the edge of town in large grounds. To the rear are a brick coach house and various smaller structures of brick and wood, including a smokehouse and what probably were slave quarters. To the right and to the rear of the side gallery are gardens and arbors and terraces, the now weedy relics of an age of formal grandeur. The house is approached through a large grove of old and very tall cedars which cast deep shade on the lichened lawn and on the curving drive which Faulkner has broken with ruts, so as to discourage people from coming to see him. Here he has lived with his wife, Estelle, their daughter Jill, and in earlier years with Estelle's son and daughter by a previous marriage, both now grown and married and living elsewhere.

It seems to a visitor that Oxford, the house, and the physical aspect of Faulkner himself are a continuum, that they have the organic relationship of a bird in a tree in a woods, or a frog on a log in a swamp. The town in turn is organic to the state, and Mississippi, undoubtedly, is organic to the South. Faulkner in his setting is thus like a good if romantic painting, in which every element is conceived in proportion and with harmony of line and color.

This conception, to be complete, needs a family: for the sense-of-family is deeply felt in the South, and is a separate dimension. Faulkner's mother, "Miss Maud" Falkner (William early in his career added the "u," reverting to the original form of the name, which had been changed by his great-grandfather), is a spry, engaging little woman of about eighty, an enthusiastic amateur painter, church-goer, and at the same time the greatest admirer of the writing of her oldest son "Billy." She lives in a comfortable house on South Lamar Street, the principal street of the town, where "Billy" generally goes to see her every day.

Down the street from Miss Maud, fronting on the square with its fine old domed and porticoed white courthouse, is the law office of Judge Falkner, Billy's Uncle John Wesley Thompson Falkner II, the brother of his dead father. Uncle John has a son, J. W. T. IV, who is U. S. marshal of the northern district of Mississippi. The intervening numeral belongs to John Wesley Thompson Faulkner III, William's brother, who is also a novelist (*Men Working, Dollar Cotton, Chooky*), and who changed the spelling of the family name to agree with William's when he, too, began to write. To avoid confusion, he is known as "Johnsie." He lives on University Avenue with his family. A third brother, Murry C., known as Jack, lives in New Orleans, where he is an FBI man; a fourth brother, Dean, was killed in 1935 while barnstorming in a plane that belonged to William. Along with these immediate relatives, William Faulkner also has numerous first, second, third and fourth cousins in and near Oxford, such as Mrs. Bob Williams, a first cousin whose husband is a former mayor of the town. In addition, through Estelle, who comes from one of Oxford's old and leading families, he is related to many other people. Thus it can be seen that the roots twine and interweave, and that the family, too, is organic with the town, the house, and its occupant.

All of this can be observed or is a matter of record. Where the continuum breaks is in the character and personality of William Faulkner himself. He prefers to be an enigma and one can believe that he will always remain one, even to himself, for his inconsistencies pass artistic license. His is not a split personality but rather a fragmented one, loosely held together by some strong inner force, the pieces often askew and sometimes painfully in friction. It is to ease these pains, one can guess, that he escapes periodically and sometimes for periods of weeks into alcoholism, until his drinking has become legendary in the town and in his profession, and hospitalization and injections have on occasion been necessary to save his life. After one of these episodes he returns for a relatively long period to an existence of calm sobriety: he is not an alcoholic, but perhaps more accurately an alcoholic refugee, self-pursued.

The war within can be seen in many aspects. He is thoughtful of others, and oblivious of others; he is kind, and he is cruel; he is courtly, and he is cold; he is a philosopher at large who has no integrated philosophy; he loves the South and feels revulsion for the South; he is a self-effacing but vain man who longed for recognition and rebuffed it when it came; a man of integrity who has contributed to a false legend about himself. Of more serious importance, he is a great writer and a bad writer. His best work ranks with the best in the world, and his worst ranks, if not with the worst, then with the merely mediocre, with the potboilers and self-conscious effusions of experimental art—"flag pole sitting," as he had called it—which he (or one part of him) scorns.

One of the virtues of Faulkner's best work is its sense of the past, so that every event is seen in deep perspective, colored and shaded like a forest floor, where today's growth feeds and blooms on the refuse of the past and will itself become food for the future. This derives from his own sense of the past: the past of the South, of his county and town, and especially of his family. For the Sartoris family, whose exploits and agonies occupy one novel and one volume of short stories and who appear as leading or supporting characters in many of the other works, have a basis of reality. They are, in fact, the Falkners (or Faulkners), as seen from William Faulkner's point of view and as molded by him to suit the needs of fiction.

Like any contemporary Sartoris, William Faulkner can be comprehended only in relation to far-off events, not simply those of his own childhood, but of generations preceding. He is the product and to some extent the victim of circumstances whose beginning can be dated in 1839 with a scene of characteristic Faulknerian violence.

2

ADVENTURES OF THE OLD COLONEL

In 1839—so the story is told in the Faulkner family—William Cuthbert Faulkner, his great-grandfather, then aged fourteen, quarreled with his younger brother James, bloodied his head with a hoe, and was so severely whipped by his father that he ran away from home (this was in Missouri, where the family had migrated from Tennessee and before that, in an earlier generation, from South Carolina). Sleeping in culverts and haystacks, begging his food at farm kitchens, hitching rides when he could, but traveling mostly on foot, he came at last to his destination, Ripley, Tippah County, Mississippi, where he had an uncle, a schoolteacher named John Wesley Thompson. There he learned that his uncle was in jail at Pontotoc, two counties away, charged with murder.

He had arrived late in the afternoon, just as dusk was falling. While he sat on the steps of Benjamin Anderson's tavern, dirty and tired and sunk in discouragement, a little girl of about six named Elizabeth Vance noticed him and asked if she could be of help. He answered that he would like a glass of water. She ran next door to her home to get it and told her mother about the "little old tramp boy." The mother went to investigate, and upon learning his name and why he was there invited him in, for she and her husband were friends of Thompson's. They fed him and washed his clothes, and next morning sent him by stagecoach to Pontotoc. But the little girl felt a proprietary interest in him, and as he was leaving she began to cry. It is related that young William embraced her and said: "Never you mind, Lizzie. When you grow up, I'm a'comin' back here and get you and *marry* you!"

At Pontotoc his uncle arranged for the boy to be fed and lodged until the trial was over. During his time in jail Thompson studied law, and when the time came acted as his own counsel. He was acquitted—and returned to Ripley as a lawyer, in time becoming a circuit court judge. He took his nephew into his home and treated him as his son.

For the next four years William attended school and worked part time in the local jail as a general handy man for the sheriff. When he was nineteen, a passing stranger named McCannon waylaid the Adcock family, who were moving from the town, killed them with an axe, and made off with their horse and carriage and two slaves. Young Faulkner helped capture McCannon, then helped rescue him from lynching; wherefore McCannon in gratitude confided the whole story of his life. Faulkner enterprisingly wrote it up in the form of a little booklet and sold 2,500 copies on the day of the execution, earning $1,250.

Not long afterward the Mexican War broke out. He volunteered, along with seventy-six other young men of Ripley and Tippah County, and was elected first lieutenant of the "Tippah Volunteers." They were not called to Mexico for a time, however, and when finally they were incorporated into the Second Mississippi Rifles and arrived at the scene, Mexican resistance in the north had been broken at the Battle of Buena Vista. Thus they never were in combat; but there were perils enough in the diseases of winter encampment at New Orleans and later during their occupation duties in various Mexican towns; and in a mutiny which ended only when the Ripley company and one from nearby Panola, Mississippi, had leveled their rifles and were ready to fire on their dissident neighbors. Also, in what apparently was an accident, Lieutenant Faulkner was wounded. The circumstances are obscure, but that the wound was suffered in line of duty is indicated by the fact that the government paid him a disability allowance until the time of the Civil War.

Afterward, back in Ripley, young Faulkner "read law" in his uncle's office and shortly joined him as a partner in practice. In 1847 he married a Knoxville girl named Holland Pearce. And in 1849 began a queer, muddled series of events that for several years were to give his life a quality both Kafka-esque and Faulknerian.

As nearly as can be made out, this trouble began when Robert Hindman, who had been second lieutenant in the Tippah Volunteers, applied for membership in a local secret society of which Faulkner was a member. Faulkner spoke in his favor, but the opposite was reported to Hindman, who thereupon violently upbraided him for his supposed treachery. In the argument Hindman pulled his pistol and fired at Faulkner's heart. The pistol misfired. He aimed again, and again the gun misfired. He cocked for a third time but Faulkner had drawn his knife, and before the trigger could snap he stabbed Hindman dead.

The next regular session of the court lay many months away, and during this time the town divided into bitter factions. In this interval Holland Pearce died in childbirth (the baby, a boy, lived and was named John Wesley Thompson Faulkner), immensely compounding Faulkner's anxieties and filling him with grief and a sense of doom. Thomas Hindman, Robert's younger brother, was studying law. At the trial, he made his first court appearance with an eloquent and bitter speech for the prosecution. Yet, when the facts were brought out, the jury had no trouble in seeing that Faulkner had acted in self-defense and he was acquitted. No sooner had he stepped from the courthouse than he was set upon by Thomas Hindman, and the struggle at once attracted partisans. In the melee, Faulkner shot and killed a man named Morris, a friend of the Hindmans.

Now almost the whole town turned against him. He was brought to trial within a few days. Again he was acquitted. Going to the dining room of the Ripley Hotel, he encountered Thomas Hindman, who drew his gun. It slipped from his hand and struck the floor; a bullet hit the ceiling. Faulkner drew his own gun and covered Hindman, commanding him to let the gun stay where it lay, and announcing to the room that he wanted no more bloodshed but stood ready to defend his life.

How much all this gun-slinging may have stemmed from Faulkner's own hot temper (evidently he was overbearing in the way that some small men are—he stood only about 5 feet 7 inches), and how much from the equal impetuosity of the Hindman brothers cannot be calculated. The family legend paints Faulkner *sans reproche* and the attempt on him as inexplicable, and the testimony of impartial witnesses in calmer times favors this view. Nevertheless, the feeling against him was so bitter that he left town.

But he came back soon and the vendetta commenced again: once Faulkner had to disarm a friend of his who was preparing to shoot Hindman. At last a duel was arranged between the two principals. It was to take place by the Mississippi, with only one witness and no doctor, and with each man armed with two pistols, shooting at will while advancing from fifty paces. Somehow the witness, a Colonel Galloway, effected a compromise before the duel could occur. Hindman soon left Ripley to settle in Arkansas, where in due course he made a brilliant political and military career.

While this imbroglio was spinning to its near-tragic end, there had been a reunion of the Tippah Volunteers with a grand Virginia Reel ball. Faulkner, as the ranking officer, was asked to lead it. The young lady selected to lead it with him, a former resident of Ripley and at that time "a distinguished guest" from Pontotoc visiting relatives in the town, was Elizabeth Vance. And so again he met "Lizzie," grown up and a beauty.

They fell in love and, as the Hindman affair finally came to a close, were married.*

Here, obviously, is material for a family legend, particularly a legend embellished in the Southern fashion, filled out with detail and colored in the telling and retelling until it assumes the flavor and dimensions of a saga, or even a myth. But great-grandfather William had at this stage barely begun his career—the legend would grow and grow.

With the outbreak of the Civil War he raised a volunteer regiment, the Second Mississippi Cavalry, and rode off at its head to take part in the first Battle of Manassas. Evidently he was a daring soldier, but the same hot temper that had started his adventures remained unchecked and he made enemies among his men. At the yearly election of officers they chose another leader and demoted him from colonel to lieutenant colonel; whereupon he rode back to Ripley, raised another regiment of volunteers—the Seventh Mississippi Cavalry—and galloped off, again a colonel, to serve with gallantry under the command of Nathan Bedford Forrest.

* The courtship inspired Faulkner to poetry:

I learned the art at beauty's college;
I am in love clear up to my nose,
And want to marry so bad I'm nearly froze;
When I lay down at night my thoughts are busy
With the phantom of my angelic Lizzie;
When in Morpheus's embrace I'm sleeping
Her image comes around my pillow creeping.

Afterward he came back to his law practice and took a leading part in the reconstruction of Ripley and its surrounding Tippah County. And soon—by 1868—he had conceived the idea which was to dominate the rest of his life, and which eventually would cause his death. He decided to build a railroad to link Ripley with the commerce of the middle South, up to Middleton, Tennessee, and with that purpose enlisted a partner named Richard J. Thurmond, a local banker and lawyer. Four years later the road—the "Ripley Ship Island and Kentucky"—was finished. It was hardly a Northern Pacific—a narrow gauge line of 60 miles, with rolling stock for only two trains, and in later years was known affectionately as "The Doodle Bug" —but while smaller than it is made to seem in the Faulkner family annals, it still was a bold venture considering the times and circumstances. With his prosperous law practice, his political interests (he had helped organize the American Party, or "Know Nothings," in Mississippi), and his distinguished military record, it established Colonel Faulkner unquestionably as one of the state's first citizens.

Probably it was about this time—the family records are not clear—that he changed the spelling of his name. There were, so the story goes, "some no-good people named Faulkner down around Pontotoc" and, as Colonel Faulkner's prestige grew, so did his irritation at being asked if he were related to them. Finally he dropped the "u," becoming Falkner, to put an end to it.

To this full life he added authorship. In 1880 he produced *The White Rose of Memphis*, a melodramatic novel in which some of the events of his early life, particularly the Hindman affair, were related in elaborate disguise. First serialized in the *Ripley Advertiser*, then published as a book, it became one of the great popular successes of its era: it sold 160,000 copies and ran through 35 editions, and was reissued again in 1952. Two years later he wrote *The Little Brick Church*, a novel laid in pre-Revolutionary New York. In 1884 he brought out *Rapid Ramblings Through Europe*, an account of his impressions and adventures during a trip abroad the previous year. (While in Italy he commissioned and briefly posed for a heroic statue of himself, which subsequently was set on a high pedestal to mark his grave; the cemetery is near the railroad, and the statue was placed so that the one monument stares out over the other). He wrote these books, his essays and letters-to-the-editor, and a great quantity of personal correspondence, usually at night, in his office, with his faithful body servant Nathan to whisk the flies and supply him with the bourbon whiskey which he consumed in large amounts. He often worked well past midnight and then, to relax his mind and body for sleep, frequently bowled for half an hour or so on the alley he had set up in his front yard, with Nathan as pin boy.

Writing was only a pastime, however. The railroad remained his preoccupation, becoming finally almost an obsession. In 1887-1888 he and Thurmond had extended the line south to Pontotoc, and his ultimate goal was Gulfport, far to the southeast. Thurmond objected, and, as he was equally strong-willed and short-tempered, their argument developed into a rancorous feud. It finally was agreed that they would draw lots, the winner to buy out the loser at the latter's own price. Thurmond lost. Falkner was a rich man, the owner of a 1,200-acre plantation, a saw mill, a grist mill, a cotton gin, and a number of small farms, and had a substantial bank account besides. Even so, it seemed nearly impossible that he could meet the extravagant figure Thurmond demanded. But he sent couriers around the town and county to all the members of his old Seventh Cavalry, and from their small private caches, from fruit jars, strong boxes, and secret chimney recesses came enough so that, together with the money he could borrow in New York against his own half-interest, he could meet the payment with less than a thousand dollars to spare. Soon afterward he ran for the state legislature so that he could steer a rate-increase bill through its course.

Thurmond filed against him for the legislature and lost. A few hours after the election results were announced, Falkner was passing Thurmond's office. Just outside the door he was stopped by several of Thurmond's henchmen who, they said, wanted to congratulate him. He chatted with them for a few moments and then (according to the Faulkner family version) turned to see Thurmond standing inside the open doorway leveling a pistol at him. The shot struck him in the mouth, and the ball lodged in his throat. It was 5 P.M., November 5, 1889. He died the next day.

Thurmond was tried for murder but pleaded self-defense, and produced witnesses to swear that Colonel Falkner had drawn first. The trial resulted in acquittal. Thurmond moved to North Carolina, where he made a new fortune in textiles.

William Faulkner's readers will have no difficulty in identifying Colonel Falkner as the Colonel John Sartoris of *Sartoris, The Unvanquished* (a collection of Sartoris stories), and various other novels and stories. His life is laid out in close detail—the first volunteer regiment, the demotion, the new regiment, the railroad, the shooting, and so forth—colored and modeled, naturally, in the interests of fiction and magnified to heroic proportions, so that Colonel Sartoris becomes the quintessence of his time and class; yet perhaps no more magnified in the fiction than in the Faulkner family, among whom, a friend has observed, "The Falkner men are always the heroes and the Falkner women the heroines of their own stories." Colonel Falkner had been dead eight years when his great-grandson and namesake was born. He had been enshrined long since as a household deity, and on the evidence of the books and stories was among the strongest influences of William Faulkner's life.

3

TO JEFFERSON

William Faulkner descends from him through the line of John Wesley Thompson Faulkner, the only child of Holland Pearce.* He was known as "the Young Colonel," an honorary title which, it is explained in the Falkner family, he "inherited" from his father, who is referred

* By Elizabeth Vance he had five children, three girls and two boys. A story told by Falkners of the present generation illustrates some features of the Old Colonel's mind, of his times, and of the native material from which William Faulkner has been able to draw his macabre humor, that strangely inverted humor of violence and bloodshed seen in *Spotted Horses,* for instance, and throughout *The Hamlet* and several other novels. The story deserves the rich Mississippi dialect unreproducible in type.

Henry, the younger son, had been paying attention to the wife of a local jeweler, who at last came to the Old Colonel and said, "Colonel, I'm afraid I'm goin' to have to kill Henry."

"I'd hate for you to do that," the Old Colonel observed. They talked it over, and the Old Colonel arrived at a solution by sending Henry to Texas to start a new life. But there he lost his money in a crap game and headed back to Ripley, where he again took up with the jeweler's wife. The jeweler at last reluctantly took action. Afterward he came to the Old Colonel and said, "Colonel, I hate to have to tell you, but I had to kill Henry."

"That's all right," the Old Colonel said. "I guess I'd a had to kill him myself sooner or later."

to as "the Old Colonel." John Wesley Thompson Falkner married Sallie Murry and had three children, a girl named Holland and known latterly as "Antee"—pronounced "Aunt T"—a boy named John Wesley Thompson Falkner (J. W. T. II, now Judge Falkner of Oxford), and Murry. The latter married Maud Butler of Oxford and became the father of four sons, among whom the first was William Faulkner, born on September 25, 1897, at New Albany, Union County, about 35 miles from Oxford.

How the Murry Falkners moved from New Albany to Oxford, an event of considerable importance in literary history—since otherwise, presumably, the Jefferson of the stories would resemble New Albany and would be populated by a different cast of characters—forms still another saga of Sartoris-Falkner derring-do. As it is related in the family, a druggist named Walker made a slurring remark about "Antee," and this was brought to the attention of Murry. Encountering Walker on the street, Murry slapped him across the face and informed him that he would come to the drug store that night to thrash him. When he arrived, he went first to buy a headache powder from a clerk; then, turning to look for Walker, saw him standing behind him with a raised pistol. Walker fired and Murry was hit in the mouth, exactly as the Old Colonel had been, even losing the same teeth. He fell to the floor, whereupon Walker emptied both barrels of a shotgun into his back.

His father, the Young Colonel, was in Oxford (the family had moved there from Ripley after the Old Colonel's death) but galloped to New Albany when he heard the news, cornered Walker in a hardware store, grabbed the lapels of his coat with one hand (lifting him from the floor, it is related), and with the other jammed a horse pistol in the scoundrel's middle. Walker pled for his life. The Young Colonel pulled the trigger—a misfire. He pulled it again—another misfire. Walker struggled and prayed to no avail. But the next four shots misfired also and Walker, managing to break free and draw his own gun, relievedly shot the Young Colonel.

Somehow, in spite of all the gunplay no one was very seriously wounded, and because of this, and the court's inability or unwillingness to fix the blame in an affair of honor, all parties were allowed to go unpunished. At this point Murry's wife, Miss Maud, made the historic decision. There had been enough shooting, she said, and if they stayed in New Albany there was sure to be more, so she was moving the family to Oxford; and she did.

The first home there was a fine old house on Van Buren Avenue, with stained glass in the windows and huge oak trees in a long expanse of green lawn. When

William was about five they moved to a house on South Lamar, a few doors away and across from the Young Colonel's mansion; near also to the house where Miss Maud now lives; and near the Oldhams, whose eldest daughter Estelle was to become William's youthful sweetheart and later his wife. In this house he passed his boyhood, and for the most part these years seem to have been unexceptional. He was rather quiet and he liked to read. But he played baseball too—he helped organize a team and became captain of it—and roamed and fished and hunted in the woods and fields. His most frequent playmates were his younger brothers and his cousin Sallie Murry (Antee's daughter), and, being older, he could manipulate them into scrapes and predicaments that have passed into the family lore. There was the time, for instance, when he persuaded them to put their tongues to an iron hitching rack in freezing weather, whereupon, of course, they all got stuck in a row. And another time when he convinced Johnsie that he could fly by using wings made of corn shucks. Johnsie took off from a second story window "and liked to killed himself." Once, roaming on his own, he shot pedestrians with a water pistol full of "stink water" from the gallery of his uncle J. W. T. II's second-floor office, and was kept home from the circus that day because of it.

He was a fair-to-good student, but liked to draw pictures in his books, and drew them so well that the family predicted that he had inherited an "artistic bent" from his grandmother Butler (Miss Maud's mother, an amateur sculptress) and would turn out to be a painter. But his own ambition was different, and evidently was formed while he was very young.

When the teacher would ask the children to stand up and tell the class what they wanted to be when they grew up—Leo Calloway, Faulkner's seat mate in the third grade, now a rural mail carrier, remembers that his answer was always the same—Billy would rise and say, "I want to be a writer like my great-granddaddy."

And, looking back now, his family can see, as J. W. T. II says, "He never was nothin' but a writer." The quality that is called creativeness in a writer is closely akin to lying, and in turn to what in children is called "imagination." Billy was a storyteller of such precocity that even then he could use the gift to avoid unpleasant work: his playmates did his chores while he entertained them. His cousin Sallie remembers, "It got so that when Billy told you something, you never knew if it was the truth or just something he'd made up." Perhaps the real world and the world of imagination have never since that time been really separated in Faulkner's mind.

This imagination could not fail to be deeply stirred

by the stories of the Old Colonel; nor, later, could it be unmoved by the contrast between the present and the past, a contrast not only in the physical aspect of the land and forests, and not only in the spirit that marked the Old Colonel's time and his own, but in the situation of his family. The Young Colonel (who was, more or less, the elder Bayard Sartoris of the stories) was a venerable figure of Faulkner's childhood, a dignified and also an exceptionally stubborn man of whom it has been said, "When he was sot, a meetin' house wasn't no sotter." He improved and extended the railroad, and branched out in Oxford as a local capitalist, becoming president of the First National Bank. When he lost control of it to a shrewd back country financier named Joe Parks (Bayard's loss of the Sartoris bank to Flem Snopes is mentioned in several stories), he withdrew all his money and, so the legend goes, put it in a water bucket and carried it across the courthouse square and deposited it in the rival bank. He was a heavy drinker; and periodically he would order his bags packed, mount his fine carriage, and be driven off by his Negro body servant Ned to the Keeley Institute for the "cure." He was chivalrous, honorable, and brave, but for all that, he was by no means the man his father had been.

In his younger son Murry, William Faulkner's father, the fire that drove the Old Colonel had burnt itself almost to an ash. The old instincts were there, as evidenced in the affair of the caddish druggist, but they were enfeebled. He dropped out of his class at the University of Mississippi (Ole Miss), worked fitfully at a number of jobs, and finally became a conductor on the family railroad. This was his job at the time William was born. After the move to Oxford he went into the livery business and ran a stable for ten years. Then he spent eight years in the hardware business. Finally, in 1918, he was appointed secretary and business manager at Ole Miss (the campus adjoins the town of Oxford) and held that job until his death. He was a kind, good-humored man who made a living and had some admirable qualities. On the other hand, he was not even a pale carbon of his grandfather, and the circumstances under which he and his family lived differed greatly from the aura of physical and spiritual grandeur in which the Old Colonel had moved.

Looking around him at other Oxford families William Faulkner could see that this was not unusual, that what had happened to the Faulkners evidently was part of a larger socio-historical event. To a considerable extent, his books seem to be an attempt to grope through to an explanation of that phenomenon.

4

THE ARTIST AS A YOUNG MAN

Naturally, this perception came later, and then only gradually. In fact, while his books do form a pattern, and eventually he came to see his work as a unity, there was no such purpose in his conscious mind during the early part of his career. Actually, he started out to be a poet. He had begun as an adolescent to write verses and at the same time other symptoms of poetic inclination set in: he became rather shy, dropped out of competitive sports, took less interest in his studies, avoided courses that did not interest him, and as a result never did acquire enough credits to graduate from high school. He read a good deal, mostly books from the Young Colonel's library, with no selectivity and no serious purpose, and spent the rest of his time mooning over his verses and strolling in the country-side. It was at this time, when he was seventeen, that he met the living person who was to have the most important effect on his career.

Philip Stone, then twenty-one years old, was a scion of one of the old families of Oxford (probably the De Spains of Faulkner's stories). His father, General Stone, was a lawyer and a prominent political figure in the state, and planned for Philip to join him in his law firm, as his older son had done. Already he had graduated from Ole Miss and taken another B.A. at Yale, and was preparing to study law at Ole Miss before returning to Yale for a second law degree as well. This tandem education was the result not only of an extraordinary precocity but of his father's wish that he have the benefits peculiar to both Northern and Southern education. Thus, by the time he encountered Faulkner, he was twice a B.A., a sophisticate who had traveled to the North, had seen New Haven and New York, and was, moreover, a literateur.

Indeed, the law as a career was less a choice than an inherited obligation. His real enthusiasm was for letters, particularly for poetry. When he heard that little Billy Falkner, of whom he had been casually aware before—the families were friends, but four years was a big difference in age—had developed into a poet, he was curious to see the result. Besides, it would be a favor to Miss Maud, who had told his mother that Billy didn't know what to do with his verses, or whether to try to do anything, because nobody in Oxford knew much about poetry or what you do with it. And so one Sunday afternoon at the Falkner house Billy got out the verses and Stone read them.

Stone remembers that he was surprised and, beyond that, excited. Not that the poetry really was very good, but, he says, "Anybody could have seen that he had a real talent. It was perfectly obvious." Forthwith he became Billy's literary mentor, and later on, as Billy grew up and the age difference faded, his closest companion and friend. The "influences" on a writer are hard to estimate, but certainly William Faulkner owes as much to Stone as any great writer has owed to any teacher, editor, or friend.

To his elementary and eclectic education Stone added at least the outlines of liberal knowledge, both orally (Stone has an oral gift, and a memory that enables him to recite whole pages verbatim) and through reading courses. First came poetry: Shakespeare, Swinbourne, Keats, Shelley, and the modern Imagists; then the standard classics, such as Balzac, Thackeray, Fielding, Defoe, Dickens, and Conrad. Joyce, in whose style and techniques one can see antecedents of Faulkner's own, was then entirely the property of the *avant garde.* But Stone passed *Ulysses* on with the comment, "This fellow is trying something new. This is something you should know about." Faulkner would read, and then they would talk about it, although Stone did most of the talking. Brilliant, facile, mentally and physically quick, Stone was a perfect complement to his taciturn, often morose younger friend, who for years accepted willingly the position of protégé.

But it was not only literature they talked about. Stone, who had a severe childhood illness requiring that he spend several years in bed and lead a quiet life for several years thereafter, had during that time developed an intense interest in the history of the old South and the Civil War. Both his grandfathers, numerous great-uncles, and removed cousins had fought in the War; there was consequently a great amount of family lore about it, and to the sickly boy their adventures and those of Lee, Jackson, Forrest, and the other leaders were vicariously his own. He grew up with this same romantic enthusiasm. And so the two friends also talked about the old South, the War, its aftermath, and the decline of one way of life and the rise of another. Again Stone was the teacher: for Faulkner, immersed though he was in family and local legend, had only a sketchy knowledge of the history of those years, and although his emotions were strong his ideas were unformulated. The picture of the South that he later projected in his stories began to evolve during those long country walks with Stone. Indeed, probably the whole Sartoris conception—and unquestionably the

Snopes conception—grew from these conversations, which took place over a period of years.

By 1918 Stone had gone back to Yale for his second law degree. Faulkner, remaining in Oxford, was trying to get into the Army Air Corps. But he was turned down because he was too short. From Stone he learned that the R.C.A.F. wanted volunteers and that he could qualify by its physical standards. So he joined Stone at New Haven for a few months, sharing his room and working at the Winchester arms factory, meantime schooling himself in British mannerisms and a British accent in the belief that he would have to palm himself off as a British subject. In this improbable disguise he presented himself to the R.C.A.F. recruiting officers, who accepted him without questioning his nationality. Soon he was in flight training. But the war was over before he was commissioned.

He had yearned for personal combat, for an opportunity to emulate those valorous actions of the legendary past. What reality could not offer, imagination contrived. His stories of young Bayard Sartoris flying in France, valiant but (like all Sartorises) haunted and doomed, and some of his other war stories, such as *Turnabout*, are as vividly felt as if he had actually been on the scene.

In the personal legend that has grown up about William Faulkner, imagination has been equally resourceful.

It is an accepted biographical item that he served with the Canadian air corps in France and was wounded in action. It is sometimes added that he was decorated for gallantry. Actually his commission was made effective only when he had returned to Oxford after the war, and he received his officer's pips through the mail. His wound consisted of a leg injury suffered when he and another cadet pilot got drunk on Armistice Day, stunted a plane over the field, and landed upside down through a hangar roof.

It has also been authoritatively told that Faulkner's homecoming marked a turning point in his career: that the returning warrior then saw his native South with a fresh eye, and fell to brooding over its condition and the splendid past. But this also seems unlikely. Idealization of the past was not a spontaneous event but a growing, even hereditary thing, like the Young Colonel's title. At any rate, it was some time before he made any move toward the creation of what would be the Yoknapatawpha saga. He continued to regard himself as a poet and turned out poetry, largely under Imagist influence, at a great rate. Then, after a while, he began to write short stories, with the practical object of making money to support himself while he wrote poems. Stone's secretary would type them and send them off, but they were invariably rejected, and they collected in a filing cabinet in the musty little red brick building occupied then, as now, by the Stone law firm. He lived at home and thus had few expenses: for spending money he borrowed here and there, mostly from Stone, and then would do carpentry or house painting or some other odd job to pay his debts and have a little extra to keep going.

By then Murry was working at Ole Miss, and his job as business manager allowed him the free use of a house on the campus. Propinquity and the belated realization that an education could be useful to him as a writer combined to send William briefly to the university as a special student. Professor Calvin Brown, head of the Department of Romance Languages, and his family lived across the street in another of the university's houses. The two families became friendly, and William, perhaps because of a lack in Murry of intellectual attainments or scholarly interests, seemed attracted to Professor Brown and often dropped in informally to talk with him about school subjects and how he could best use his time at the university. Professor Brown is dead now, but his wife, who also had been a teacher, remembers that "Billy seemed to be faltering and groping his way at that time. One day, I remember, he told my husband that he felt his thinking was fuzzy and wondered whether studying mathematics would help him. My husband said he certainly thought it would, and so Billy enrolled in a math course. He seemed quite interested the first few weeks, but then he began cutting classes more and more and finally just drifted away. He seemed to be the same way in most of the subjects he took. He was a gentle, nice boy, quite shy and sensitive, and always courteous. He was wonderful, too, with children. He's always liked children and known how to talk with them, tell them stories, and get along with them; they respond to him. That was an outstanding characteristic I remember from those times, and the other was his intellectual groping." (A bit later, his liking for children and the outdoors combined to make him Scoutmaster of a local troop of Boy Scouts, but the Baptist minister objected to his drinking and he had to retire.)

He took part in some of the school affairs, even buying a full dress suit so as to cut a good figure at school dances (this evidently had slipped his mind later, when his New York publishers bought him a dress suit to wear at the Nobel presentation; "I'm just a farmer," Faulkner said. "I never had on one of these monkey suits"). He did a number of ink drawings for the school annual, quite creditable imitations of John Held Jr.'s "flappers and sheiks" then in style. He spent a good deal of time at the library, reading Stone's choices and browsing curiously through all sorts of subjects, acquiring miscellaneous information that he would make use of later in his writing. He would say many years later,

"It's not just Faulkner sittin' there at the typewriter and lickin' the postage stamp to send the manuscript off to some publisher. It's a thousand men livin' and dead." But the rigidities of formal education offended him. His only good marks were in French and Spanish. He failed in English and dropped that in his second semester, and finally, early in his second year, left school altogether.

Afterwards he reverted to his previous activities, writing more poems and stories, which collected at such a rate that finally they filled a filing cabinet in Stone's office; working at odd jobs; getting drunk occasionally when he had the money; riding around with Stone in the latter's convertible "Drucilla" during off hours and on weekends; visiting Memphis now and then (the great bordello scenes in *Sanctuary* were one result); lounging around the courthouse square listening to the old-timers there—the farmers and hunters and stockmen—swap their stories of local characters and Indians and carpetbaggers and Negroes and famous hunts and how things were in the old days. "Mississippi isn't a state; it's a club," a local aphorism says, meaning that everyone knows a good deal about everyone else, usually for generations back. Faulkner was almost as taciturn then as he is now, but what the old-timers wanted was not a conversation but an audience and he was collecting material that would turn up later in many stories.

Meantime he seemed to be getting no place, and his personal oddities were such that the town began to regard him not only as a loafer but as a sort of mild lunatic. He grew a beard, wore old, dirty clothes, and in the summer often went without shoes. He would appear at "Mack" Reed's drug store on the square, his bare feet perhaps grimy from a long, solitary walk in the fields and woods, "hunker down" on his haunches by the magazine rack, and read the latest periodicals oblivious of the paying customers who came and went. Reed, whose dead younger brother had wanted to be a writer, and who thus felt a sympathetic interest, never bothered him, and periodically helped him with the loan of a $10 gold piece with the understanding that he would change it at the bank and later redeem and return it; and Faulkner always did so. His manner was equally peculiar: he might stand for hours gazing at the old courthouse, or walk about in the town in a distracted manner, lost in some impenetrable private reverie, seeing no one and replying shortly, and sometimes rudely, if some old friend or former teacher spoke to him. "He was the real poet-type," a townsman remembers.

The town was used to expecting the unexpected from the Falkner family, who were famous for a self-assurance that made them oblivious to the opinions of others, and the common explanation of William's behavior was,

"It's the Falkner in him." On the other hand, the Falkners were proud, aristocratic, and were considered rather snobbish. The news of William's full dress suit, spreading like wildfire, had been considered typical of the way the family "put on airs." The anomaly that he now presented was irresistibly a subject for humor, and the town wits had soon invented a nickname for him, "Count No'count."

Except for Miss Maud, Stone was the only one who believed that some day he would be successful and famous (Murry's native tolerance was wearing thin). Faulkner himself, though endowed with at least a normal measure of the family trait of self-confidence, which in his case sometimes seemed closer to arrogance, had begun to doubt that he was really cut out to be a writer, or in any case that he would ever get recognition as one. Stone suggested that he try New York, where he might meet some editors and critics and be able to interest them in his work. Stark Young, who had grown up near Oxford and had taught at Ole Miss, lived there. He had already interceded at Ole Miss to enable Faulkner to attend as a special student, and could be counted on, through his literary connections, to be helpful in the big city. So in 1923 Faulkner arrived in New York and, accepting Young's invitation to stay with him, picked up odd jobs (one was washing dishes in a Greek restaurant) until Young was able to get him a job clerking at Scribner's Book Store, which was managed by Young's friend Elizabeth Prall.

Meeting Miss Prall, as it later turned out, was the one useful result of the trip. He made no headway in the publishing world, and six months later, hearing from Stone that the university postmastership was open and that he could have it (Judge Oldham, the family's former neighbor and father of Estelle, was a Republican and dispensed federal patronage), he was glad to come back home.

He was not a success as a postmaster. The mail piled up, the hours of opening and closing grew vague, the records became confused or lost, the customers' complaints were met with silence or abuse, while Faulkner drank, wrote poetry, and took long walks. Once, after receiving complaints from parents and prospective students that their requests for the school's catalogue were not filled, the official in charge investigated and was told by Faulkner, "Oh, that's second class mail, so I just throw it over in that sack and wait 'til the sack's full before I send it." Stone used his political influence to keep him from being fired, but finally Faulkner yielded to popular demand and quit anyway, with the comment, "Now I won't be at the beck and call of every son of a bitch who happens to have two cents."

Afterward he returned to his old life, taking on only enough odd jobs to keep in spending money. His uncle

J. W. T. II remembers, still with a sort of mild astonishment, "He just *wouldn't* work." The postmastership had given him ample opportunity to work on his poems, however, and afterward Stone subsidized the private printing of a collection of them, his first published work, called *The Marble Faun*. It received little attention and only a few copies were sold.

5

SHERWOOD ANDERSON, FLAUBERT, AND POPEYE

Stone then had another idea. T. S. Eliot, Ezra Pound, and several other native poets had made their reputations in America by first making them abroad, and he suggested that this might work equally well for Faulkner. The idea appealed to Faulkner, who was curious in any case to see the French battlefields. So in January, 1925, the two friends set off for New Orleans, Stone for a holiday, Faulkner to get a job on a Europe-bound ship. But such jobs were hard to find. Stone returned to Oxford, Faulkner stayed on in New Orleans. One day he learned that Elizabeth Prall was in town with Sherwood Anderson, whom she had recently married. Faulkner called on her and thus met Anderson, whose work he admired greatly. They became good friends and, according to Faulkner, this led directly to his first novel, *Soldier's Pay.*

"Sherwood and I used to walk around together and sit drinkin' and talkin' together until three or four in the mornin'," he has recalled. "He was one man I know that I could have shared a desert island with. We would have got along.

"He never did any work, as far as I could see. I'd tried a little writin' myself, poems and just amateur things. I suppose I was like everybody else: as soon as they learn to spell they start to think about composin'. But I'd never worked much at it. Lookin' at Anderson I thought to myself, 'Being a writer must be a wonderful life.'* So I disappeared for six weeks and the next time I saw Elizabeth she said to me, 'Where have you been? Sherwood's missed you.' I said, 'I been writin' a book.' She said, 'Would you like for Sherwood to read it?' and I said, 'Not particularly. I know he's busy.' " Mrs. Anderson passed this information on to her husband who sent word back, according to Faulkner, that in return for this courtesy he would recommend

* In 1953, Faulkner wrote an "appreciation" of Anderson for *The Atlantic,* in which he reported a different version: "During those New Orleans days and weeks, I gradually became aware that here was a man who would be in seclusion all forenoon—working. Then in the afternoon he would appear and we would walk about the city, talking. Then in the evening we would meet again, with a bottle now, and now he would really talk; the world in minuscule would be there in whatever shadowy courtyard where glass and bottle clinked and the palms hissed like dry sand in whatever moving air. Then tomorrow forenoon and he would be secluded again—working; whereupon I said to myself, 'If this is what it takes to be a novelist, then that's the life for me.' "

the book to his publisher, Horace Liveright, who was expected to be in New Orleans shortly.

Liveright duly arrived, was told by Anderson about his "discovery," read the manuscript, and agreed to publish it. Faulkner was elated. He settled into the life of the French Quarter, where Anderson presided over a little Bohemia of artists and writers, contributed to their official journal, *The Double Dealer*, and sold some short stories to the New Orleans *Times-Picayune*, which thus has the distinction of being the first organ of any sort to publish his fiction. He also wrote most of his second novel, *Mosquitoes*, a satire on the dilettantes who cultivated the group. Both novels were, in a sense, potboilers: the first a disillusioned story of a war veteran who comes home to die of his wounds, a theme and treatment manufactured under the strong influence of the currently popular Hemingway-Dos Passos school, the second an awkward attempt at the sort of social comedy then being brilliantly produced by Aldous Huxley. Also, and unfortunately for his relations with Anderson, he collaborated with William Spratling in producing a little book called *Sherwood Anderson and other Famous Creoles*. Spratling, who at that time was teaching architecture at Tulane, and who later became famous for reviving the native art of silverworking at Taxco, Mexico, making that place a great tourist attraction, did the drawings for the book, and Faulkner wrote the text. He composed the introduction in Anderson's own literary style, and although the intention was good-humored, Anderson's feelings were hurt by what he conceived to be a cruel parody. He refused to see Faulkner again; and they met only once more, several years later, at a cocktail party in New York.

Unhappy though its ending was, the association had permanent influences on Faulkner's life and work. Anderson was a dedicated man with an almost holy respect for the art of writing. In the years to come Faulkner, amid many adversities, would show this same impermeable dedication, the same striving to "do the best you know how to do," the same urgent conviction that the telling of a story, and the way it should be told, were very important matters. And, as he has written, "I learned that, to be a writer, one has first got to be what he is, what he was born; that to be an American and a writer, one does not necessarily have to pay lip-service to any conventional American image such as his and Dreiser's own aching Indiana or Ohio or Iowa corn or Sandburg's stockyards or Mark Twain's frog. You had only to remember what you were. 'You have to have somewhere to start from: then you begin to learn,' he told me. 'It don't matter where it was, just so you remember it and ain't ashamed of it. Because one place to start from is just as important as any other. You're a country boy; all you know is that little patch up there in Mississippi where you started from. But that's all right too.' " Faulkner did not follow this advice at the time, as the two novels written in New Orleans show. But it stayed with him, and it was on the basis of such precepts—whether exactly remembered from Anderson or not—that he finally reached maturity and effectiveness as an artist, an event foreshadowed in *Sartoris,* the next book he wrote.

In spite of turning out two books in six months, Faulkner was not too busy to take part in the diversions of the time and place. There was congenial company; for during one of those spontaneous migrations that pull artistic personalities to a given locale, the French Quarter had become a seed bed of talent. During the mid-twenties the changing group included Roark Bradford, Oliver LaFarge, George Milburn, George Marion O'Donnell, and Hamilton Basso, to name only the best known alumni, and especially during Anderson's stay attracted such wandering stars as Carl Sandburg, John Dos Passos, and Sinclair Lewis. Few of the young men were making a living at writing, and in their mutual poverty and mutual admiration for Anderson, who usually invited three or four of them to his home for Saturday night supper, a camaraderie was established. Basso, a native of New Orleans, was there during the whole period and remembers Faulkner as "a small man, with beautiful manners, soft-spoken, with great courtesy" and "very conscious of being a Southerner." Faulkner lived for a while in a downstairs room in a street off the Cathedral, near Spratling's attic; and from the latter, Basso recalls, some of the young literati once staged a footrace over the rooftops of the Quarter. Prohibition was felt as a personal challenge by all and there was a good deal of drinking, but Faulkner took no more than most of the others. The group was never formalized, but members drifted in and out of Spratling's attic and tended to meet two or three times a week for dinner at some inexpensive restaurant. Although there was some literary discussion, such occasions served mostly for companionship and light-hearted high jinks. Basso recalls that once, with elaborate fanfare, Anderson was served with a piping hot brick.

Faulkner made his greatest impression on his friends one night when he appeared at dinner, looking much pleased with himself, and announced that he had spent the whole day in the air with the Gates Flying Circus, a barnstorming outfit that had settled temporarily near the city, and had been allowed to do some wing-walking (the Gates Flying Circus contributed to Faulkner's later novel on barnstormers, *Pylon*). By his later recollection, he also did some rum-running, piloting—he wrote—"for pay a power launch belonging to a boot-

Phillip E. Mullen

'e photo by Nina Leen
yright Time, Inc.

In Faulkner's world, which closely resembles Oxford and its surrounding Lafayette County, each landmark takes on a symbolic quality. The jail (above) and courthouse (left) are inanimate characters in many stories, especially in *Requiem for a Nun.* The town square (below), first a scene in *The Sound and the Fury,* reached a poetic apotheosis in *Intruder in the Dust* twenty years later.

Life photo by Walter Sanders
copyright Time, Inc.

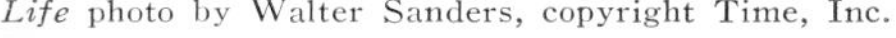

Life photo by Walter Sanders, copyright Time, Inc.

Life photo by Walter Sanders, copyright Time, I

Three generations of Falkners: (left, above) William Faulkner's great-grandfather, the Old Colonel; (right, above) his grandfather, the Young Colonel and his wife; and (below) Murry, his father, as painted by "Miss Maud."

Phillip E. Mullen

fe photo by Walter Sanders, copyright Time, Inc.

Life photos by Nina Leen, copyright Time,

William's close relatives in Oxford include his mother, "Miss Maud" Falkner (above); his Uncle John, J. W. T. Falkner II, shown (above, right) in his law office; Uncle John's son J. W. T. IV (below, right), U.S. Marshal of the northern district of Mississippi; and William's brother "Johnsie," J. W. T. III (below, with William), who writes novels and has taught writing at Ole Miss. The Falkner family proliferates as far as Nashville and New Orleans.

illip E. Mullen

On a trip to Europe in 1925, Faulkner stayed in Paris for a while and took on the coloration of the Left Bank (right). Some six years later, with the sudden wealth from *Sanctuary,* he was able to indulge the passion for flying that he had acquired in the RCAF. He owned several planes but lost interest after his brother Dean, barnstorming in one of them, was killed near Pontotoc.

Day and Bruner

Day and Bruner

Sanctuary's success also enabled him to buy the old Shegog house at the southern edge of town, one of several identical mansions built in Oxford before the Civil War. It has extensive grounds and adjoins fields which Faulkner also owns. Faulkner has a study filled with books and decorated with his guns, where he writes when he "feels like it," most often very early in the morning.

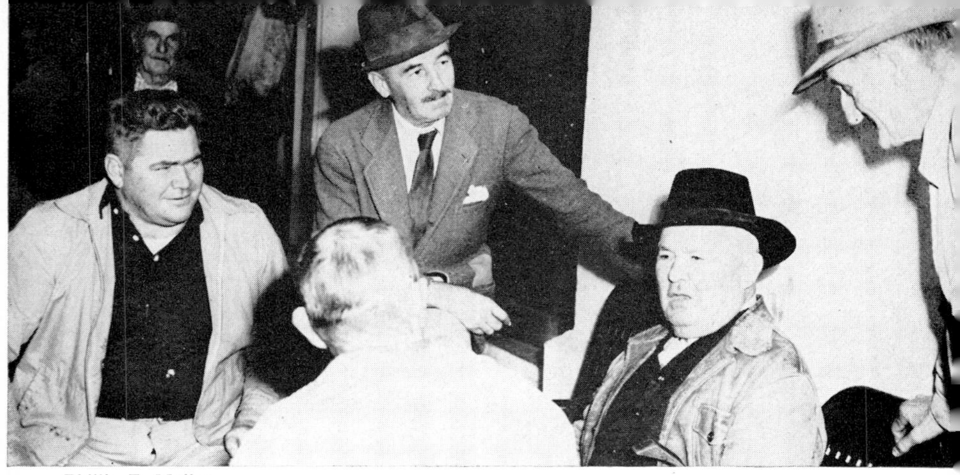

Phillip E. Mullen

The annual hunt in Sharkey County is directed by "Uncle Ike" Roberts. Here "Uncle Ike" (second from right) is seen at his usual headquarters, outside the Colonial Hotel, chatting with some of the regular members. Right: Mrs. William Faulkner, the former Estelle Oldham. Below, Faulkner talks over old times with Phil Stone in Stone's law office.

Day and Bruner

Life photo by John Dominis, copyright Time, Inc.

At an MGM cocktail party before the première of *Intruder in the Dust,* Faulkner submitted uneasily to being interviewed and photographed.

Phillip E. Mullen

A devoted father, Faulkner helped arrange parties for Jill (in white dress, above). She accompanied him to Stockholm: at right, they are seen entering the plane. Below: Faulkner at the Nobel Prize ceremonies.

Wide World Photos, I

Life photo by Cornel Capa, copyright Time, Inc.

legger . . . taking the launch across Pontchartrain and down the Rigolets out to the Gulf, the Sound, then lying-to with no lights showing until the Coast Guard cutter . . . made its fast haughty eastward rush, going, they always liked to believe to Mobile, to a dance; then by compass to the island . . . where the Caribbean schooner would bury the casks of green alcohol which the bootlegger's mother back in New Orleans would convert and bottle and label into Scotch or Bourbon or gin. . . ."

Faulkner finally left for Europe in July, 1925, landing first in England, then taking a walking and cycling trip through France and the Low Countries, where he closely inspected the battlefields, the old air bases, and the villages which by then had been peaceful for eight years. While abroad he received a $200 advance on *Soldier's Pay* from Liveright, the first substantial money he had earned from ten years of writing. He was able to stay on for awhile on that, and to see parts of Italy and Switzerland, and by the time he came home *Soldier's Pay* had been published. But it sold poorly, and later, when *Mosquitoes* was issued, its sales were little better. Liveright, who had signed him to a three-book contract, repented his judgment and canceled it. Faulkner meantime had been able to sell a few short stories, but the pay was small. He had thought himself finally launched as a writer, and he was bitterly disappointed.

In *Sartoris,* which he now wrote, he turned for the first time to subjective and local materials. The hero, young Bayard Sartoris, is to some extent a projection of Faulkner's romanticized picture of himself, and both the Old Colonel and the Young Colonel make their first fictionalized appearances. But the dedication, the deep urge to "do the best you know how to do," had not fully developed. The theme—the juxtaposition of modern times and modern men with men and times preceding, to the disadvantage of the former—was a serious one and, in fact, basic to most of his later work, but Faulkner's interest in exploring it was equalled by his desire that the book please the popular critics and sell well to the public. The compromise showed; it was not a particularly good book. It lodged in the vaults of Harcourt, Brace and Company, who showed little interest in actually publishing it.

It was under these circumstances that Stone, as he recalls, finally proposed a new approach to which Faulkner, from his association with Anderson and through the maturing of his own taste, judgment, and self-awareness, was now completely receptive. Since Faulkner was not equipped or at least seemed not destined to be a "popular" writer, Stone urged, why not forget about trying to please the public and write simply for himself and for those readers of taste who surely would some day recognize his talent? "I had in mind Flaubert," Stone has said. "Instead of catering to an audience he wrote for the ages, and of course the ages discovered him."

This noble purpose would be compromised later on, one example, ironically, being in the Gavin Stevens stories (collected as *Knight's Gambit*) whose leading character was modeled considerably on Stone himself. These and some others were written for "the market." But the immediate result of Faulkner's decision was a book of spectacular literary "purity," entirely without commercial intent and entirely drawn from his own deepest resources. It was *The Sound and the Fury*, a brilliant book, perhaps the most impressive he has ever written. But it is also the most difficult to read, with the first section the babblings of an idiot, the second the stream-of-consciousness impressions of a neurotic on his way to suicide, and only the last in easily comprehensible form. It was published in 1929 by Harrison Smith after Harcourt, Brace had finally brought out *Sartoris* with neither financial nor critical success. *The Sound and the Fury* was an instant *success d'estime*. Although ignored by the public it accomplished what was now Faulkner's goal, to be admired by "the discriminating few," as Stone said, in the hope that their taste eventually would form the taste of the intelligent many.

This was also the year that Faulkner was married to Estelle Oldham. He had been in love with her for years, but she was two years older than he, which was one difficulty; his eccentricities and lack of prospects were others; both families disapproved. Finally she had married a lawyer named Cornell Franklin, who took her off to live for awhile in Honolulu and later in Shanghai. Then in 1927 she had divorced him and come home with her two children, a boy and a girl, to live with her family in the old home on South Lamar Street. Faulkner soon was paying court to her again. He still had no money—and in fact had to borrow his part of the wedding expenses—but she had had a small income settled on her, and with two books being published, a third, *As I Lay Dying*, nearly done and his demonstrated ability to live as a jack-of-all-trades, this did not seem too great a hindrance. They were married in the College Hill Presbyterian Church and moved with the two children into a small apartment. Faulkner took up the awkward role of husband, father and good provider.

As I Lay Dying was finished—Faulkner says that he wrote most of it on the back of a wheelbarrow in the university powerhouse, where he was firing boilers—and proved like *The Sound and the Fury* to be a critical success but a poor money maker. Then came *Sanctuary.*

Faulkner himself has said of it that it was "a cheap idea, deliberately conceived to make money," and considering both the book itself and his personal situation, that is easy to believe. On the other hand, the idea had been in his mind for a long time, it was something that he wanted to do, and he took it seriously, at least in part, when he was writing it. The result of what probably were mixed motivations was a mixed book, part wonderful, part second rate.

Sanctuary was a tremendous popular success. Faulkner spared almost no details in developing the highly sexed plot, and the public stampeded to buy it. Magazine editors wrote to him; Hollywood wanted him. He and Stone sat back in amazed delight—but only momentarily. Then they opened the filing cabinet, the old manuscripts were dusted off and retyped, with a large price in the upper right corner of each title page, and sent off to the same magazines that had rejected them before. The money poured in.

Sanctuary sold even in Oxford, where Mack Reed stocked it, as he had the earlier books, out of friendly sympathy for Faulkner. But people usually wanted it wrapped in brown paper so as not to be seen with it. The whole town was scandalized. Even Professor Calvin Brown was dismayed, and demanded of his wife, "Now, why would *anybody* write a book like *that?*" Murry was as shocked as anybody. Crossing the campus one day he saw a co-ed he knew with the book and urged her not to read it, because "it isn't fit for a nice girl to read." Cousin Sallie Murry chided Faulkner directly, saying, "Now you *know* you weren't raised that way." Estelle's family was taken aback, too, and Faulkner, in a rare moment of what was interpreted as contrition, explained to Dorothy Oldham, his sister-in-law, that he "had it to do," that he felt he had to do something to make money and that she shouldn't read the book, that when he wrote a book for her to read he'd bring it to her (later he brought her *The Unvanquished*).

But the dam had been broken. In Oxford and the world at large he had made his name mean something. Famous or infamous, he could no longer be ignored. He had begun—in a phrase he would use many years later—to make his "scratch on the face of anonymity."

6

THE MATERIALS OF THE MYTH

Faulkner had invented Yoknapatawpha (Yawk-na-pa-*taw*-pha) County and Jefferson in *Sartoris*, and in the subsequent three books had filled in many geographical and historical details. The rest of his career has been devoted largely to an exploration of that not entirely mythical domain. *Light in August* (1931), *Absalom, Absalom!* (1936), *The Hamlet* (1940). *Intruder in the Dust* (1950), and *Requiem for a Nun* (1952) are the other major pieces in the series, which also includes a novelette—*The Bear*—and many short stories. Of these, a number of the best have been collected under the titles *The Unvanquished* (1938) and *Go Down, Moses* (1942). The whole work has often been compared with that of Balzac; and it is true, at least, that there is a similarity in scope. Balzac set out to describe the France of his era, not simply aspects of it but as a social panorama. The world that Faulkner describes is not less complex. If its dimensions are smaller, it is only because he has used his imaginary Mississippi county as a microcosm in which he has laid the story of the whole South, as seen from his peculiar point of view.

On the other hand, whereas Balzac created a tapestry in which every scene has a planned relationship to every other, Faulkner's work is less a tapestry than a *collage*, an assembling of many diverse and often seemingly unrelated elements, put together by intuition as well as deliberate intent, until almost by accident the separate parts have merged into a meaningful unity. If the separate items seem oddly proportioned, and the whole effect seems unstable and irrationally marked with gaps and protuberances, it is because Faulkner did not at all set out to do what he has done. It was not until he had written many stories and several books that it dawned on him that what he was writing was, in effect, one book—what he now calls "the book."

The discovery did not cause him to draw up a Balzacian master plan. Trusting his intuition, he wrote those stories which seemed to him at the time to have most interest and meaning, letting the *collage* grow, often doubling back in time to supply earlier episodes, to which existing episodes thus became sequels, leaving gaps to be filled someday, starting sagas and putting them aside to start others, brooding over this private world, not so much its creator as the medium through which it was trying to be created. It has been a method eclectic, pragmatic, intensely private, and essentially poetic.

And it is as a poet (a kind of anti-Wordsworth) that he can best be comprehended. Just as Yoknapatawpha County is not a literal place but a place in his mind, so his "plots" are not reportage but the subjective, almost unconscious impressions that he has formed of the real region which Yoknapatawpha represents. In this corporeal bit of the South and its particular past, a past which in every way influences the present, lie the materials of the artist.

The past so pervades Oxford and Lafayette County (pronounced La-*fay*-ette locally) as to make them somehow seem very old, older than places in Virginia and the Carolinas which far pre-date them. Mississippi was admitted to the union in 1817; even then only the southern third had been settled by white men. The rest was Indian country, and it was not until 1832 at Pontotoc (where eight years later the future Colonel Faulkner, as a boy of fourteen, would come to find his jailed uncle) that the Chickasaws signed the treaty that opened the whole area to white settlement. The event brought an influx from the Carolinas, Tennessee, Virginia, and Alabama, including the founders of Oxford (among these Robert Shegog, the original owner of the house now owned by William Faulkner). Lafayette county was created in 1836, a 679-square-mile section of pine-covered hills bounded on the north by the Tallahatchie River and on the south by the Yocnany River, which in those times was called the "Yocanapatafa." The year previously, an Indian trading post had been opened at a site which was approximately in the center of this area, and on June 22, 1836, the county seat was officially located here, on land donated by the proprietors of the trading post, and named Oxford in the hope that a state university someday would be located there. By 1840 the county population had reached 3,689 whites and 2,842 Negro slaves. There were also a few Indians who had chosen to stay behind when the tribes, by the terms of the Treaty of Pontotoc, had agreed to move to Oklahoma Territory.

Like all frontiers, this one in northern Mississippi attracted young, ambitious men, the majority of them still single, few of them well educated, affected with the common idea of establishing themselves and if possible becoming rich. The symbol of wealth and success, an almost universal dream, was the plantation—the great farm-estate with its big house, its animals, its outbuildings and numerous slaves. The dream made men work hard and plan big; it also brought land speculation and the aggressiveness and frequent violence of frontier boom times—what were known in retrospect as "the flush times." The code of behavior of the era was recalled many years later in his memoirs by Reuben Davis, captain of the Tippah Volunteers when young William C. Faulkner was that organization's first lieutenant:

"People had not begun to write about muscular Christianity in those days, but they understood and practiced it. Their creed was generally simple. A man ought to fear God, and mind his business. He should be respectful and courteous to all women; he should love his friends and hate his enemies. He should eat when he was hungry, drink when he was thirsty, dance when he was merry, vote for the candidate he liked best, and knock down any man who questioned his right to these privileges."

Within a few decades, by the time of the Civil War, the pattern of plantation aristocracy was in full bloom. The young, rough pioneers had become landed barons in great houses and felt the need to surround themselves with evidences of that culture which few had had time or opportunity to acquire before. The houses grew ornate inside and out, with fine furnishings brought from New Orleans, New York, and abroad; the library shelves displayed Shakespeare and the standard classics; there were gilded harps and finely carved and inlaid pianos in the music rooms, where wives and daughters cultivated this among other refined arts, such as china painting, in a rapid accretion of gentility, until the whole society had become highly mannered and a chivalric tradition had grown up, no less strong for being newly established. The first William Faulkner by that time owned a large plantation near Ripley.

In Oxford, where his famous descendant would grow up, there were additional influences at work. As the founders hoped, a state university was organized there in 1848—on grounds separately incorporated as "University"—and brought a certain narrow-gauge cosmopolitanism. At the same time, in the years preceding the Civil War, the university served as a focus and sounding board where regional opinion coalesced and was amplified: the idea of secession took form early, and the tragic aftermath was perhaps the more bitter. In Oxford also was the Federal Court for the District of Northern Mississippi, bringing with it lawyers and their oblique schemes and strategies and impressive rhetoric. It was an absorbing free show they put on, and people took a great interest in the traps laid and escaped, the justice ponderously dispensed, and the theatricals of the pleadings. The Southerner seems to have a weakness for flowery oratory; here in Oxford it had perhaps an especially permeating quality, and its effects were continuous, since the court remained and is there yet.

Rhetoric—unbounded and overflowing, sometimes as melodious and syncopated and as meaningless as the transported howlings of a backwoods Negro preacher; rhetoric without internal or external logic but nonetheless emotionally stirring—later would be found abundantly in the works of the present William Faulkner.

The plantations, the university, the court, and the vigor of a newly founded feudalism combined in Oxford to make a thriving and richly patterned society. It produced some great men. A. B. Longstreet, the future confederate general, was president of the university from 1849 to 1856. He was succeeded by F. A. P. Barnard, who left at the outbreak of the war and attained a substantial reputation at Columbia University. Jacob Thompson was Secretary of the Interior in the cabinet of President Buchanan. Lucius Quintus Cincinnatus Lamar, lawyer and teacher, eventually became Secretary of the Interior in Cleveland's cabinet. R. A. Hill, presiding judge of the court, was well known throughout the South. These and men of lesser reputation supplied a fine patina to the local civilization. But underneath lay that hot-blooded, quasi-chilvaric temperament, independent and quick to resent, described by Captain Reuben Davis, and it burst loose in 1861.

There was not a great deal of material damage in Oxford. General A. J. Smith, raiding from Tennessee in 1864, burned the town square and the house of Jacob Thompson, who was in Canada trying to enlist help for the Confederacy. Grant occupied the town in December, 1862, but did no damage; afterward General Forrest made his headquarters there and used the university buildings as a hospital, a function they had also served after the Battle of Shiloh. These events, of course, became vivid local memories. An old building on the campus is pointed out now to the visitors, and gory details of the agonies and deaths that occurred there are related. A cemetery nearby recalls how bodies by the hundreds were dumped into a common grave. Such sights—and the inevitable stone soldier on the courthouse square—were daily reminders to the present William Faulkner, and to his forebears, of the general defeat, and with a particularization natural enough the war in memory sometimes seemed to revolve around the local events. But actually the town was in an eddy of the war.

Doubtless this accounted for the surprising liveliness and industry it demonstrated afterward. It underwent the usual infestation by carpetbaggers, the usual racial antagonisms and incidents, the occupation by federal troops (1868 to 1875), and the other strains and tensions of Reconstruction, but endured them with evidently more than usual easiness, and proceeded on its course much as before. This was the period, it will be recalled, when Colonel William C. Faulkner was building his railroad, writing his books, and cultivating his various other interests nearby in Ripley. Other men were similarly busy in Oxford, among them a number of the old leaders, who had returned to pick up the threads of their pre-war enterprises.

It was not until some years later, when this generation had begun to die out, that an increasing lethargy settled over the town and county. The great men did not reproduce themselves. With increasing absorption, the town began to think of its past. The glorious events of the old days, especially the days during and before the war, loomed in the misty distance pure, brave, and out of human scale; the present, in contrast, was mundane, and its inadequacies—physical and emotional—were laid to the tragedy of the old defeat. Oxford and the South lapsed into the nurturing of a legend.

Why was this? Defeated peoples have risen again to virility, sometimes to excesses of it. Perhaps the reason lay partly in the contemporary, almost universal outmoding of the aristocratic and genteel tradition which comprised the social mores of the class of leaders, and to which their descendants clung out of sentiment and pride. Doubtless it lay partly in the gradual depletion of the land itself, victimized by corn and cotton until opportunity had been washed away in the gullies. And partly in the overpowering growth of finance and industry in the North and West, draining off both capital and human initiative, and creating a mental climate of lethargy simply by invidious comparison. It lay in all the various, inexact, and in part unconscious reasons why a society fails in its response and begins the slow retrograde process.

And this process was well along by the time of the present William Faulkner's birth, and continued during his boyhood and youth, and seems only now, in the industrialization and scientific agriculture gaining rapidly in the South, to have reached a turning point. Yet these very factors, which may contain the origins of a new leisure class and a new genteel tradition (however remote), are so antithetical to the old culture that any sensitive being attached to the latter could not help being repelled by their advance, by the substitution of the mechanical for the human element, and of the imposed for the "natural" design. Above all, such a being would be repelled by the entrepreneurs of the new design: the pushing, acquisitive, unchivalric representatives of mass man who, filling the vacuum left by the default of the old order, began to take over both political and economic power—the "rednecks" symbolized by William Faulkner as the Snopes family.

In Faulkner's books and stories there is an immense amount of observation and comment, ranging from opinions of motor cars to opinions of the universe, none of which he acknowledges as his own. "I am not responsible for the statements of my characters," he has said. "I am not responsible for anything lost or found in any pages of my books." Since, however, it is unlikely that even the most detached artist would spend a lifetime telling stories that have no significance for him, one can believe that Faulkner's interests, temperament, and beliefs are reflected in his work. And, in fact, a juxtaposition of his themes with the real events just described is the only way by which the former can be understood and made intelligible. Consider, first, the morbidity: In Faulkner's writing, life has no meaning except to the individual. There is no moral law beyond what in an older day might have been called "the code of the gentleman"—"courage and honor and pride, and pity and love of justice and of liberty"; but to keep this code brings no rewards beyond self-respect—it brings no salvation, no protection, for the "good" and "bad" characters are damned impartially to futility, and often to physical and mental tortures so macabre and so vividly conveyed that they seem to reflect sadism in the writer. The rare exceptions are made usually for "bad" people—people like Flem Snopes in *The Hamlet*—avaricious, cruel men who triumph over what, in any ordinary lexicon, would be called virtue.

Yet, while so often rewarding the "bad" and penalizing or frustrating the "good," Faulkner usually leaves no doubt as to who is who. A substantial part of his work is concerned with the theme of Sartoris *vs.* Snopes —the Sartoris family and their like, whether known by such names as Compson or De Spain, being the leaders of the old South, sometimes weak and sometimes wrong but fundamentally good, noble, and brave. It is not, however, a simple contest between good and evil, for the Sartorises themselves are stained. It was they who brought slavery to the South and this great sin, in Faulkner's mystical reckoning, has had to be expiated: their defeat in the Civil War, the ordeal of Reconstruction, the emotional and moral decadence that has overtaken them, leaving them helpless before the onslaught of the Snopeses, are all beads of penance on a rosary that has no end.

Punishment implies law, and law, a lawmaker. Faulkner has occasionally seemed to have intimations of God, but these are so vague in his work that evidently they have no relevance to any major theme of the Yoknapatawpha series. Instead, it is the land itself that has imposed the punishment. Slavery put a curse on the land, and the land put a curse on the Sartorises which can be lifted only (if ever) by generations of damnation and individual expiation. Meantime what Faulkner calls the "legal fiction" of ownership of the land has fallen to the Snopeses, who cut its forests, let its farms erode and its rivers silt, take everything from it and give nothing, until—for instance—Mississippi has become the poorest state per capita in the Union. But the land takes its retribution against the Snopeses by making them hollow men and women, as impotent emotionally and spiritually as Popeye, the Snopesian city gunman in *Sanctuary*, is impotent physically. The Snopeses eventually will come to ruin, Faulkner implies, just as the Sartorises have done, and as many Snopeses —such as the farmers who abuse their land and let it gully and wash away—have already done.

Thus the land itself, the living earth, is hero, God, and protagonist in Faulkner's work as a whole. "People don't own land," one of his characters says. "It's the land that owns the people." If Faulkner has a philosophy, this may be its distillation; although it is less a philosophy than a mystique, a religious revelation. As such it is beyond definition and beyond criticism.

7

THE MATURE YEARS

The physical Oxford has not changed greatly in the last fifty years or more. There are, of course, superficial differences: the paved streets, the cars and trucks and garages, the neon signs, some "moderne" store fronts, the real estate developments at the edge of town, but not only the spirit but most of the geography has remained intact, suspended *in vitro*, surviving without thriving. To the visitor who has read Faulkner's books, the feeling is of having awakened from a dream to find it real. Here is the old courthouse, now painted white, with its cupolas and pillars and worn steps; inside, the musty, dusty smell of history, old records, old births and deaths and marriages, old grime worn into the walls and floors until it is structurally a part of them, the very air stale; outside, on the lawn shaded by big trees and trampled in patches to hard dirt, the benches where the old men (and some young ones) come and sit in the shade and talk politics and crops, gossip, swap their stories, chew and spit and whittle and while away the years. In the summer, especially on Saturdays, the curbs are lined with sawhorse and plank trestle tables piled with produce, corn and tomatoes and rich ripe melons, quick cash crops brought in by the farmers to this informal market. The men, black and white, stand around in their faded khaki pants and worn damp shirts and wide-brimmed dusty hats, and mingle in little eddies and clusters, and serve the occasional customers with constrained movements of their wiry bodies and hard hands. The Saturday traffic moves like a slow whirlpool around the square: farm families in old cars and trucks, now and again a whole truckload of Negroes, doubling or tripling with all their children in one precarious mass in and suspended from the creaking cargo bed, sometimes a horse and wagon moving soddenly among the swifter elements. The sidewalks swarm; on the west side of the square, by long unspoken tradition, the Negroes gather, until by noon on Saturday that block is startlingly black.

Lamar Street bisects the square on the north and south. If the square is Oxford's heart, Lamar Street is the spinal axis, literally a geographical axis and spiritually the locus of many of its reflexes. Here are a majority of the fine old houses, many with broad "galleries" and imposing columns, great trees sheltering the sweeping lawns and mossy walks. These are homes worthy of the Sartorises and Compsons in their greatest days. In the web of other, nearby streets are other fine houses, some of them now badly rotted from long neglect. Otherwise one sees brick and clapboard houses in various sizes and designs, most of them in the rather fussy architecture of the late nineteenth and early twentieth centuries. Some of the streets are not yet paved. There are trees everywhere; the murderously hot summers demand shade.

Beyond the town, in spite of occasional rich farmsteads, the overriding impression is of poor land, cruelly marked by gullies, and poor, thin crops and poor people living precariously in dishevelled, paintless houses. Here the "rednecks"—so called because the sun has given their skin a permanent reddish-brown coloration—and Negroes exist. The effort of existence is itself considerable; there seems to be little left for anything else. There is a slow deliberation in the way these people walk and speak, as if they were pushing through an invisible but enveloping and heavy fluid.

In this museum William Faulkner lived and continued to write. He was part of it; it was part of him—intellectually and spiritually it was his very identity. He wrote about it with a quality of obsession, sometimes breaking off—as in *Pylon* and *The Wild Palms*—to examine other locales and themes, with indifferent results; but always returning to it, peopling his half-imaginary town and county with families, inventing a detailed history of their movements and thoughts and inter-reactions, until it seemed that he had the private affairs of thousands of characters indexed and was impeded only by lack of time from weaving them into an endless saga.

His own life during these two decades varied little from year to year. He was a kind if erratic father to the two Franklin children, and told them and their friends stories just as he used to entertain his own playmates. He and Estelle had a child whom they named Alabama, after his favorite aunt, Alabama Falkner, the Young Colonel's sister, now Mrs. Walter McLean of Memphis. This child died soon after birth, but then there was another, their daughter Jill,* and Faulkner became devoted to her. The house itself was a constant interest, and its large grounds and adjoining pasture land soon supported horses and dogs, so that with its Negro staff it soon took on the old aspect, dimmed and diminished to be sure, of baronial plantation life. The Faulkners entertained rather often, mostly members of their respectively large families, but

* Estelle, wanting a boy, had planned to name him after William. When she regained consciousness after the delivery the doctor said, "Well, you haven't got a 'Bill,' but you've got a mighty fine 'Jill.'" They used the name.

also there were friends from town. And they went out, sometimes to cousin Sallie's (Mrs. Bob Williams) farm where there was good fishing and swimming in the pond, and usually a fish-fry at night around a big fire, with Faulkner leading "Water Boy" in his high voice or perhaps scaring the children with ghost stories.

In the spring and summer there was all the activity of the farm. Bought some twenty years ago with money earned from Hollywood, it lies on Puss Kuss Creek in Beat Two (Mississippi counties are divided into "Beats") sixteen miles north of Oxford. Faulkner has formed the belief that the farm has made him independent of any other source of income, and often says, "I'm not a literary man. I'm just a farmer who likes to tell stories." Actually it is marginal land and barely supports the tenant family who operates it, but Faulkner has always taken a great interest in it, likes to string wire, dig postholes, and plan the crops, and the illusion of being a full-time working farmer evidently gives him great satisfaction.

In the fall there is hunting—especially one event so traditional that it had long since become "The Hunt," a ritual handed through generations of Oxford men and boys. It began some sixty years ago when General Stone, Phil Stone's father, and his friends made camp at "Stone's Stop" in a forest area of the delta country southwest of Oxford. Eventually the timber companies moved in, bringing civilization, a process memorably described in Faulkner's *The Bear*, and the camp site moved 190 miles south of Oxford in Sharkey County to an area of rivers, swamps, and deep forest. Around the 18th of November, Faulkner and half a dozen or so friends drive there, with a following truck stocked with equipment and food staples, and stay for a fortnight. The group varies but most often includes Leo Calloway, Faulkner's old school seat-mate, Bud Miller of the county highway department, Red Brite, a store clerk, Bob Evans, a farmer, John Cullen, a concrete worker, and "Uncle Ike" Roberts, formerly the county sheriff. "Uncle Ike"—evidently a model for the character of Ike McCaslin as seen in *The Bear* and the important short story *Delta Autumn*—is too old now to do much hunting, but acts as "camp boss" and is deferred to by all for his great knowledge of the woods and lore of the hunt. Everyone shares the work and "Uncle Ike," speaking of Faulkner, has said, "I've never seen him shirk pickin' up the smutty end of a log."

The woods have a good variety of game, including deer in plenty and occasionally a bear or wildcat. Faulkner is a good shot and as good a woodsman as any, and has such stamina that he has been known to go three nights without sleep while tracking raccoon, his favorite game. "The Hunt" has been established so long that the game warden never bothers the group. "Uncle

Ike" recalls, with admiration, watching Faulkner "pass up three does in a row without movin' a muscle."

The hunters sleep in tents and eat on a table knocked together from lumber they bring along. Venison, of course, is the mainstay of the menu, but depending on the day's luck, there may also be fried young squirrel with red gravy and biscuits, broiled or fried 'coon, "bird" (quail), catfish and "brim" from the river, or Brunswick stew, a dish that usually includes squirrel, pork, venison, okra, corn, potatoes, tomatoes, and onions and is cooked in a big kettle all day. Whatever it may be, supper is washed down with substantial draughts of bourbon and water. At night, while the pine log fire snaps and flames in the middle of the camp, the hunters sit around and play "nickel poker," read the papers that someone will have fetched from town, along with the ice, drink a good deal, and talk about the day's experiences, and other hunts, and the people they know, and the people and times their fathers or friends or wives or acquaintances knew, in a rolling tapestry of narrative and anecdote, unhurried, relaxed, and vivid and filled with the small, precise details of shrewd natural observation. Faulkner, in his stained clothes and old crushed hat, is indistinguishable from his friends except that he listens a good deal more than he talks, sitting on a log or "hunkered down" on his heels, smoking his pipe; and occasionally, unobtrusively, he scribbles a few notes. From such notes and memories have come the material for the marvelous stories that have made Faulkner, whatever else he may or may not be, one of the greatest nature writers who ever lived.

In later years Faulkner found another diversion to bring him into the middle of nature. In 1940 the government finished the three-mile-long Sardis dam on the Tallahatchie River about eighteen miles northwest of Oxford, creating a lake of about ninety square miles. A good deal of the shore line is wild country, and there are many little coves and fingerling branches. Faulkner bought a small cat boat and became an enthusiastic sailor. Earlier, he had done a great deal of flying and at one time owned two planes, one of them a big cabin model. In 1935 his brother Dean was killed in it while barnstorming from a makeshift field at Pontotoc. Faulkner, telling a friend years later about that tragedy, related how he had "put his body together in a bathtub"; the horror of that day remained, along with some disposition to blame himself for it, since the machine belonged to him, and he seldom again piloted a plane.

He and Stone continued to be good friends, but as the years went by their interests were increasingly divergent. Stone married Emily Whitehurst, an English teacher at the University High School, and they had two children, a boy and a girl. "Miss Emily" was herself ambitious to write fiction, and Stone, believing, as he has said, that he had contributed as much to Faulkner's development as he could, naturally felt a greater interest in her work. He was busy, moreover: he was becoming one of the state's leading lawyers, and in time would be the president of the Mississippi State Bar Association and a member of the House of Delegates of the American Bar Association. Finally there was little left of the earlier literary relationship. Besides being absorbed in the personal activities mentioned, Faulkner was no longer inclined to take his advice even if Stone had given it. He had come to maturity as an artist, was fully aware of his powers and supremely confident of them, and in his determination to write for himself and "the ages" (with time off for commercial writing) had become impervious to suggestion from any source.

He wrote as he lived, with an eclectic disregard for the rules, "telling himself stories," as his brother John has said, on subjects of his choice in a manner less resembling formal composition than free association. The time, place, and writing materials were unimportant; he has, he says, written on the backs of old bills, on envelopes, even on toilet paper when nothing else was handy, and his publishers learned not to be surprised to find pages of old, discarded manuscript or movie script crossed out and the reverse side used for his latest writing. Insofar as he had a routine, it would consist of getting up at about 4 A.M. (he needs only about five hours sleep) and then, if he felt like writing, working at it until about 8 A.M., typing rapidly and correcting between the lines and in the margins with a pen in a fine, small, almost illegible script. The rest of the day would be spent in the various duties and diversions arising from his property, livestock, and family, with perhaps another period of writing in the late afternoon. "Writin' has been a hobby with me," he has said. "Like collecting stamps." And evidently it has not—with an exception noted later—caused him any of the familiar torments of less facile authors. A friend who had the opportunity to watch him during several months of creation was struck by his ability to write at top speed, as fast as he can type, for half an hour or so; then to relax for perhaps another half hour with conversation or a book, preferably a mystery story; then return and type again at the same breakneck rate, perhaps picking up an unfinished phrase and continuing without hesitation. Similarly the intervals of farm work or house repairs, when his attention was occupied with practical things, evidently were the times when the actual work of literary creation occurred, almost unconsciously, so that the actual writing was mostly a mechanical act. (V. S. Pritchett, in an appropriate figure, has referred to his "agonizing prose which appears to be chewed like tobacco and occasionally squirted out, instead of being written.") Indeed, one is tempted to believe that a great part of his writing has been the product literally of his unconscious mind, that he learned to trust it as the true expression of what he wanted to say, and preserved it all because of an inability to winnow it consciously and critically. Nor would he trust others to do so. He might listen politely if an editor complained that a passage was too involved —and often they became so involved and tangential in meaning as to be incomprehensible—but he rarely would change a word.

Thus in maturity the "Count No'count" of earlier years had become, at least in many outward manifestations, a substantial citizen: a landowner, husband and father, a success in his profession. Yet, as his work shows, his personal vision of life was not modified. With "cosmic pessimism," as it has been called, he continued to paint the Yoknapatawpha landscape in bloody and somber colors, filling it with vignettes of depravity, bringing his characters almost invariably to a tragic end. At the same time he became progressively more withdrawn, as if sealing himself and his vision from any possible contamination. Fame brought attention from the world—from editors, critics, other writers, admiring readers, curiosity seekers—but having wanted exactly this, having attained it he now vehemently rejected it, and became inaccessible except to a few friends. He still appeared in the town, usually to sit on a bench on the courthouse square and listen to the endless gossip and reminiscences that went on there, or perhaps to lean against the mailbox on the First National Bank corner (the Young Colonel's bank) and, puffing on his pipe and speaking only if spoken to, gaze for an hour or two at the courthouse and the town-life that eddied around it. He even took a sporadic part in local affairs, writing letters-to-the-editor on issues that seemed important to him: such things as permitting beer to be sold in Oxford, which he strongly favored, and replacing the old courthouse with a modern building, which he strongly opposed. And during the last war he organized and headed the local air raid wardens, appointing wardens and making sure they did their duty. But he was as abrupt as ever in his ordinary manners, icy in the face of any attempt at familiarity, while at the same time, among people he liked—and especially among old people and children—he could be extraordinarily thoughtful, courteous and warm-hearted. When "Aunt Caroline," an aged Negress who had worked for the Faulkner family for three generations—and had been "inherited" by him and Estelle—died, she was "laid out," as she had wanted, in the Faulkner parlor and Faulkner himself preached the funeral oration.

The town paid little attention to him. There was an

awareness that his books were well thought of by professors and "Northern highbrows." Many of them, visiting the university, would try to meet him; but Faulkner, with what the town considered utter perversity, was never available to them. To Alicia Markova, the ballerina, he sent word back, "Please give the lady my regrets. I have a previous engagement to hunt a coon."

So far as his books were known at all among the citizenry—and *Sanctuary* continued to be the only one that was well known, until *Intruder in the Dust* came along—they were considered unreadable and a libel on Oxford and the South. The church ladies might feel pity for Miss Maud (though never to her face; "Billy" was still "the light of my life"), and the businessmen were resentful that the town's name was so often mentioned in connection with Faulkner's; but he was like a splinter lodged deep in the skin, long since healed over and only occasionally annoying.

The taciturnity, the contemplation, the appearance of aloof and unheeding purposefulness, disguised a conflict whose nature he confided to no one, but which was of such intensity that he was driven to escape. His alcoholic holidays from reality as he saw it or felt it became a necessary fixture of his life, and they grew longer and more complete. Occasionally they produced violence, but generally they were as unobtrusive as his normal behavior. He would supply himself with whiskey and, after a period of elation, retire to his own bed, drinking until sleep or coma set in, drinking again when consciousness returned, until days and nights had passed and slowly he returned to the world. At such times his friends and relatives would come and sit with him, taking turns so that he always had attention and care, as with any other serious illness.

8

HOLLYWOOD AND NEW YORK

With the success of *Sanctuary,* Faulkner had several invitations from Hollywood. A story goes that one studio baited its offer with an appeal to his chivalry, through the person of Tallulah Bankhead. The scene allegedly was Charlottesville, Virginia, where, in a first flush of enjoying his success (and before his withdrawal from all such affairs) he had gone to take part in a writers' conference. Miss Bankhead appeared, told him how much she admired his books, and asked him to come to Hollywood to write an original screen play for her. Faulkner replied: "Well now, I'd like to help a Southern girl who's climbin' to the top. But you're too pretty an' nice a girl to play in anything *I'd* write. I wouldn't want to do that to you."

Fairly soon, however, the bonanza from *Sanctuary* and his short stories tapered off. He had committed himself to big expenses with his purchase of airplanes and the old Shegog house, which needed new sills and other costly repairs. He did as much of the work himself as he could, not only to save money but because the house had become a major preoccupation for him. Indeed, he did little but work on it during many months. But one day the bank called to notify him that he was overdrawn by some $500. He came to his Uncle John (J. W. T. II) to borrow $5, explaining that he had spent his last money to wire one of the studios to accept its offer, provided it would wire him an advance so that he could square his account and be able to leave something for Estelle and the children while he was away. Judge Falkner thought that was a bad idea and offered to lend him the money he needed. But nothing could change his mind until he received the studio's wire of acceptance, which included the condition that he would have to contract for three months' work—at that, he backed off. His cousin, John, J. W. T. IV, the Judge's son, urged him not to be foolish; and after lengthy family discussions William turned his local affairs and his bank account over to John to handle in his absence, collected a few elementary personal effects, and drove to California.

Thus began a miscegenated relationship which, in spite of every nominal reason for failure, worked out advantageously for all concerned, has lasted all these intervening years, and continues now. Besides helping to adapt three of his own works—*Sanctuary,* which became *The Story of Temple Drake* (with Joan Crawford as Temple); *Turnabout,* one of his short stories about the war; and *Intruder in the Dust*—he has written or collaborated on many other films. The number is vague because in some instances, while under studio contract, he has been assigned "additional dialogue" and story "doctoring" on films that bear other writers' names. He has done such odd jobs with the equanimity of a craftsman called upon to exercise his trade, swapping his technique for money: the money necessary to support himself and his family while he applied his talent to matters that concerned him. (By 1936, five years and three books after *Sanctuary,* he was in such financial trouble that he felt it necessary to run a classified ad stating, "I will not be responsible for any bills made or debts contracted or notes or checks signed by Mrs. Wm. Faulkner or Mrs. Estelle Oldham Faulkner.—Wm. Faulkner." Reporters following up this item found him at home, helping Estelle with arrangements for Jill's birthday party. He saw no reason for their interest, he said; the ad had been "just a matter of protection until I pay up my back bills.") He has been to Hollywood about a dozen times since the first visit, working for Warner's, 20th Century-Fox, and MGM and a variety of producers and directors, but chiefly for Howard Hawks, an urbane and rather austere man who suffers from no literary hero worship but regards Faulkner as an exceptionally useful literary mechanism. Hawks has said, "He has inventiveness, taste, and great ability to characterize and the visual imagination to translate those qualities into the medium of the screen. He is intelligent and obliging—a master of his work who does it without fuss."

Useful as it has proved to be, however, the alliance has provoked wonder and some dismay on both sides. Faulkner and Hollywood have contributed to each other's legend: the result, mutually, has been a blurring of fact and fiction.

One category of stories concerns Faulkner's drinking, and these are told with some awe and implied admiration:

—the time he attended a polo match, drank too much, borrowed a polo pony and rode it onto the field, fell off, and woke up "starin' right into Darryl Zanuck's teeth bendin' over me" (so he is quoted). "It was such a feelin' of horror that I became instantly sober."

—The time they cleaned out his office after he had left Warner Brothers, and in his desk found only an empty bottle and a sheet of yellow foolscap on which he had written, five hundred times, "Boy meets girl."

—The time he hired a male nurse, whose duties were to follow at three paces with a small black bag containing a bottle, to be produced as needed, and to make sure that Faulkner reached the studio on time the next morning.

—And so on, through many variations, including such aphorisms attributed to him as "Civilization began with distillation," and "They'll never improve on Bourbon whisky," and "There is no such thing as bad whisky. There's just some whiskies better than others."

Another variety of story revolves around Faulkner's refusal to become involved in Hollywood's social life:

—The time, for example, when (it is alleged) he was at last prevailed upon to attend a party at the house of his current employer, found himself increasingly bored but, not wanting to seem rude by excusing himself publicly, went to the second floor, opened a window, and escaped by climbing down a trellis.

—The time he accepted an invitation to a party at Marc Connelly's house and his friends, thinking that attractive feminine companionship might make him more responsive to the occasion, got him a "date." After picking her up Faulkner spent the evening sitting in a chair, puffing his pipe and sipping a drink. At last the girl went to Connelly and said, "I don't think Mr. Faulkner likes me. He hasn't said a word to me all evening. I'm going home." Connelly hurried to Faulkner and asked, "Don't you like your date?" Faulkner puffed his pipe, looked up, and said, "Which one is she?"

—The time when he was invited to another party to

meet a famous woman, formerly a member of Congress and at the time in Hollywood writing a movie. Faulkner had never heard of her. When her remarkable career was related, he replied, "She don't sound like anybody I'd particularly like to meet," and declined to go.

Another kind of story hinges on Faulkner's impermeable Mississippi mannerisms and outlook:

—The time, as related by movie writer Stephen Longstreet, when "Bill, very lonely for home, had bought himself a mare and was raising a horse in Hollywood. When she was in foal he had a problem. One day leaving the studio, I found Bill sitting in his car, the very pregnant mare in a trailer attached to the car. I asked him where he was going, and he said, home to Oxford. 'I don't want any mare of mine to throw a foal in California.' And he was off for home."

—And the time (probably the most famous of the Faulkner Hollywood stories) when he grew tired of reporting to the little office assigned to him and asked his superiors if they would allow him to write "at home." The permission was given: some weeks later his employers were horrified to receive a post card postmarked "Oxford, Mississippi"—the place *he* had meant.

Faulkner's version of this incident (which may be equally fictionalized) is that when he finished his first movie assignment, Howard Hawks said, "Don't you want to stick around and pick up some more of this easy money?" But, Faulkner relates, "I had saved up about $5,000 and that was more money than anybody had in the state of Mississippi. I figured I didn't need any more right then, so I came home. Hawks said, 'Well, if you ever need any more, let us know.' After a while the money did run out, so I wired the studio I'd like to get another contract. I didn't hear anything, but pretty soon the checks started comin'. Well, that went on from November to May. Then I got a wire, 'William Faulkner, Oxford, Mississippi. Where are you?' signed by the head of the writers at the studio. I wired back, 'No message,' signed William Faulkner. A wire came back, 'Go to New Orleans and report to Tod Browning on location.' I wired back, 'Can't. Pregnant' (we were expectin' our baby soon). Wire came back sayin' I should go to Memphis an' catch a plane for New Orleans. I could just as well taken a train and been in New Orleans the next day, but I followed my orders and went to Memphis, waited around two, three days, and flew to New Orleans and reported for work.

"Browning said, 'Get a good night's sleep so we can get an early start in the morning.' So I did and next morning everybody took off for the bayous where they were doin' the picture on location. By the time we got there the sun was goin' down, so we turned around and came back. Went on like that for a while. I asked Browning when I was supposed to start to work, and what was the story? Browning said I should go see the continuity writer and ask him. I found him, introduced myself as the dialogue writer, and said, 'What's the story?' The continuity writer said, 'Never mind about that, you go off and write some dialogue and then I'll tell you what the story is.'

"So I went to Browning and said the continuity writer wouldn't tell me what the story was. Browning said, 'Why, that son of a bitch. You tell him to tell you the story right away.' But before I could, there was a wire from Hollywood sayin', 'Faulkner is fired.' Browning blew up and said, 'Never mind'—he'd fix that. But then there was another wire sayin', 'Browning is fired.'

"Meantime, though, they had built the set. What they decided they wanted was one of those old Cajun shacks out in the swamps on stilts. They could a' bought the finest example in the state for fifty dollars, but that wouldn't do—they had to build one for about a thousand dollars. While they were buildin' it and hammerin' away on it, an old Cajun came along in his canoe and sat there in the water in the hot sun all day long just watchin' and studyin' what was goin' on. Next day he brought back his whole family in canoes and rowboats, grandmothers, babies, and all, and they all sat there watchin'.

"After Browning was fired the whole thing broke up and everybody went back to Hollywood. But, you know, the last time I was in New Orleans I went out to look at the place, and the Cajuns were still comin' to look at that set and puzzle over it."

Faulkner's indifference to the diversions of the movie colony was simplified by the fact that until he received the Nobel Prize, relatively few of the movie people had a clear idea of who he was. Except among the writers and a section of movie intelligentsia (among whom culture has superseded the older snobbery of Cadillacs) he was known, if at all, as a "writer": a "famous" one, no doubt, but still, within the local hierarchy of values, a person of only moderate consequence. A rather typical point of view, perhaps, was expressed by Preston Sturgis, a playwright and movie writer of some celebrity, who as a sideline owned and operated a restaurant-*cum*-Little Theater called the Players Club on Sunset Boulevard. Faulkner, having been taken there by a friend, found the atmosphere congenial and in due course was introduced to Sturgis. Politely, Faulkner said, "I hear you've made some very fine pictures." Said Sturgis, with equally good manners, "I hear you've written some very fine books."

Faulkner did not care for Hollywood and predated Evelyn Waugh in the discovery that death is a major preoccupation of its inhabitants. This was interesting to him, he once told a friend, because of his feeling that it was, for him, a kind of purgatory, a place where it was necessary to come from time to time to do penance. He has accepted this necessity, however, with good humor, leading, as nearly as possible, the kind of life with the kind of companionship that he would ordinarily lead at home in Oxford. His friends have included a bartender, a haberdasher, a painter, and some writers and other movie workers to whom he has been attracted by their human qualities—such men as Gene Fowler, Nunnally Johnson, Joel Sayre, Al Bezerides, Edmond Cohn, and Al Pogano. One tells what it is like to be a friend of Faulkner's: "We sit around together—he'll be smoking and pulling on his pipe—and maybe not say a word for ten minutes at a time. Then one of us may say something, and we'll talk awhile, and then sit awhile. Or I may be talking, and he'll put a word in here and there; or he may tell a story, and when he does tell one he tells it with a wonderful sense of anecdote. When he drinks he talks a lot, and sooner or later he'll want to recite *The Phoenix and the Turtle*, his favorite Shakespeare. He likes to live and eat modestly. He always stays at some small, inexpensive hotel and he eats in small, inexpensive restaurants, mostly at Musso Frank's. When he's here we have a sort of routine: a few drinks, then dinner with wine, generally at Musso's, then take a walk, and then to a quiet place for a nightcap, and then he goes off to bed. When he leaves town you never hear from him, he never answers letters, but when he comes back you take it up right where you left it with him. You learn never to ask him about his books or what he's working on because he doesn't want to talk about that. He's always calm, always polite, a little bit formal, very courteous. I've never seen him get mad except when some brassy type tries to move in on him and get palsy. Then he freezes up, withers the guy, and moves away from there." Faulkner's intense reserve makes him seem colder than such friends know him to be. Stephen Longstreet has recalled, "I was part of a car pool that picked him up every day outside his hotel and he rode every day with four or five movie writers who were too scared to talk to him. It was at the end of one of these rides that one of the screen writers said to me, "He must like you, Steve, he said 'good morning' to you."

Faulkner's dislike of becoming personally involved with the movies was carried to extreme lengths in 1949, when MGM decided to film *Intruder in the Dust* in the natural setting of Oxford and Lafayette County. The town was thrilled: the arrival of director Clarence Brown, his crew, and the cast caused more excitement than any visitation since General A. J. Smith's raiders, and for two months Oxonians delightedly formed themselves into street scenes at Brown's request. An ironic touch occurred when a mob was supposed to storm the local jail in an attempt to lynch Lucas Beauchamp, the old Negro who is the central figure of the story. There had been just such a scene some years before, ending in a real lynching; and some of the same men who had taken part in it joined now, with movie-struck enthusiasm, in the make-believe version. Everyone wanted the chance to "see yourself in the movies."

Faulkner took a good deal of interest in the movie and worked closely with Brown on technical details and choice of locales. But when the filming was done and the "world premier" approached, he refused to be involved in that event at all, to the dismay both of MGM's promotion department and of his own family. Cousin Sallie Murry's husband, after all, owned the Lyric Theater where the premier was to take place. But Faulkner would not even pose for a photograph to be put on the billboard. MGM arranged a luncheon in his honor and invited all the members of the local civic clubs; but Faulkner excused himself on the grounds that he would be "runnin' my school bus" at that hour, picking up Jill and some neighbor children from school to take them home for lunch, as was his custom. Nor did he plan even to attend the Lyric on the great night. He had given away his tickets, he said. Emery Austin, the MGM publicity man in charge, enlisted Estelle's help but she, even with Jill's earnest support, could do nothing to change his mind.

Austin meantime had spent several weeks building

his program to appropriately collosal size. An 8-million-candlepower searchlight was set up in the courthouse square. A "mammoth parade" was organized, with both the high school and Ole Miss bands marching, and with director Brown awarding $350 in MGM prize money to the best floats entered by local and university clubs. The Chancellor of the university would entertain "dignitaries"—the Governor was scheduled to be among them—at his official residence at dinner. There would be a World Premier Ball at the university gymnasium and a monster rally in the public square, the latter lit by one-million candlepower of spot and flood lights as well as the great searchlight. Brown and the stars of the cast would speak; Freddie Burns and his popular string band would make the music for street dancing, with "Esmeralda, nationally known radio and recording hill-billy style prima donna and comedienne" as a special attraction. Brown would present Mayor Williams with a placque to be hung in the city hall "as a permanent expression of MGM's appreciation of the city's help" during the filming. Editors and movie critics from all over the South would be flown in; the newsreels would be there; the whole affair would be broadcast over two radio stations. It was going to be tremendous. The only missing element was the author, who remained invisible and immovable.

At last Estelle had a desperate inspiration: she telephoned Aunt "Bama" in Memphis. A matriarch of powerful opinions, she is known in the family as the only person in the world who can "really manage" her nephew, who regards her with mixed humor, affection, and awe ("When she dies," he has commented, "either she or God has got to leave Heaven, because both of 'em can't be boss"). Aunt Bama called Faulkner and, it is related, informed him that she was on her way and that he would have to escort her to the premier because "I've waited a long time to be proud of you and I want to be there when you take your bow." Moreover, she was wearing a fine dress for the occasion and he had better be dressed up.

And that is the way it happened that Faulkner attended the premier, dressed up and escorting Estelle, Jill, and Aunt Bama.

The other occasional center of Faulkner's activities has been New York, where he has had to come from time to time to see his publishers and which, in any case, seems to furnish him relief from the tensions that sometimes assail him in Oxford. In New York, as in Hollywood, he has lived modestly and quietly, seeing a few chosen friends, spending his days usually at his publisher's office, writing or working on proofs, remaining aloof from the social paraphernalia that attracts a good many writers living in or visiting in New York, and at rare times joining one of the semi-social gatherings with which the publishing business abounds. As in Hollywood, his austerity of manner and intolerance of aggressive good-fellowship have left some bruised feelings. One time, a friend who was there recalls, a famous publisher appeared at a literary soiree to which Faulkner had been enticed, and upon being introduced launched an effusive speech telling Faulkner how much he admired his work. He had a collection of them, the publisher went on to say, and had brought them along that day and would be honored if Faulkner would sign them. Faulkner listened without expression, puffing on his pipe, and when the man had finished answered curtly, "I only sign books for my friends."

It had not been many years since Faulkner had come to New York to stay with Stark Young, clerk in Scribner's book store, and had tried to attract the notice of some publisher—almost any would have done. Among the discoveries he had made in the interval was one that, as he has said, "Literary people bore me. They're the dullest people in the world. I haven't read any of their books and I don't want to talk about mine, so that leaves us nothing to talk about."

9

THE ARTIST AND THE CRITICS

His attitude toward "literary people" had some relationship to the reception that his books received among many of them. After the first burst of admiring, if somewhat puzzled, applause at the appearance of *The Sound and the Fury* and *As I Lay Dying*, a majority of literary critics had become progressively dismayed by his subsequent work. *Sanctuary* confirmed as a major Faulknerian theme the morbidity that lay beneath the technical brilliance of these two earlier important books; and as the other novels came along, and no sign of a moral purpose could be seen in them, Faulkner was accused of being the leader of a "cult of cruelty," an exploiter of vice and violence for its own sake, a writer lacking spiritual or literary responsibility. To this, the leftist critics—in an era when they were many and influential—added the charge of political irresponsibility: for, with all the poverty and depravity that Faulkner described, he never indicated that there might be an answer (or even that an answer was needed) in social action. Others suspected that he might even be planting seeds of Fascism. As Maxwell Geismar wrote: "For it is in the larger tradition of reversionary, neo-pagan, and neurotic discontent (from which Fascism stems) that much of Faulkner's writing must be placed—the anti-civilized revolt arising out of modern social evils, nourished by ignorance of their true nature, and which succumbs to malice as their solution."

Faulkner's obscurity was also attacked. What Faulkner himself has described as "writing on the oblique, seein' the thing through reflections," and Conrad Aiken has spoken of as "the whole elaborate method of *deliberately withheld* meaning, of progressive and partial and delayed disclosure," was called by Clifton Fadiman a method of "Anti-Narrative, a set of complex devices used to keep the story from being told . . . as if a child were to go to work on it with a pair of shears."

His style, which Aiken described as "like a jungle of rank creepers and ferocious blooms taking shape before one's eyes—magnificently and endlessly intervolved, glistening and ophidianly in motion, coil sliding over coil, and leaf and flower forever magically interchanging," was viewed by a majority with less favor. Bernard

De Voto said that "When a narrative sentence has to have as many as three parentheses identifying the reference of pronouns, it signifies mere bad writing and can be justified by no psychological or esthetic principle whatever." Others called his style "indecent," "perverse," "second rate," the reflection of a "slipshod and redundant artistic machine." Joseph Warren Beach commented: "Half the time we are swimming under water, holding our breath and straining our eyes to read off the meaning of submarine phenomena, unable to tell fact from figure, to fix the reference of pronouns, or distinguish between guess and certainty. From time to time we come to the surface, gasping, to breathe the air of concrete fact and recorded truth, only to go floundering again the next moment through crashing waves of doubt and speculation." Alfred Kazin spoke of "perhaps the most elaborate, intermittently incoherent and ungrammatical, thunderous, polyphonic rhetoric in all American writing"; even Aiken called the style, "all too frequently downright bad."

The critics' (not to mention the general reader's) impatience can be understood from this sample, a passage from *The Bear:*

". . . Not enough of even Father and Uncle Buddy to fumble-heed in even three generations not even three generations fathered by Grandfather not even if there had been nowhere beneath His sight any but Grandfather and so He would not even have heeded to elect and choose. But he tried and I know what you will say. That having Himself created them He could have known no more of hope than He could have pride and grief, but He didn't hope He just waited because he had made them: not just because He had sent them alive and in motion but because He had already worried with them so long; worried with them so long because he had seen now in individual cases they were capable of anything, any height or depth remembered in mazed incomprehension out of heaven where hell was created too, and so He must admit them or else admit his equal somewhere and so be no longer God and therefore must accept responsibility for what He himself had done in order to live with Himself in His lonely and paramount heaven. And He probably knew it was vain but He had created them and knew them capable of all things because He had shaped them out of the primal Absolute which contained all and had watched them since in their individual exaltation and baseness, and they themselves not knowing why or how nor even when: until at last He saw that they were all Grandfather all of them and that even from them the elected and chosen the best the very best He could expect (not hope mind: not hope) would be Bucks and Buddies and not even enough of them and in the third generation not even Bucks and Buddies . . ."

From this same story, here is an example of this same

style disciplined and effective: "Then he saw the bear. It did not emerge, appear: it was just there, immobile, fixed in the green and windless noon's hot dappling, not as big as he had dreamed it but as big as he had expected, bigger, dimensionless against the dappled obscurity, looking at him. Then it moved. It crossed the glade without haste, walking for an instant into the sun's full glare and out of it, and stopped again and looked back at him across one shoulder. Then it was gone. It didn't walk into the woods. It faded, sank back into the wilderness without motion as he had watched a fish, a huge old bass, sink back into the dark depths of its pool and vanish without even any movement of its fins."

Faulkner's style and content have been the subject of endless scholarly analysis. The best as well as the shortest analysis may well be that contained in an interchange between him and his cousin Sallie Murry Williams. She asked, "Bill, when you write those things, are you drinkin'?" and he answered, "Not always."

In 1939, especially with essays by George Marion O'Donnell, Warren Beck, and Aiken, and soon in other pieces by Delmore Schwartz and Robert Penn Warren, a more sympathetic interpretation began to emerge. (V. S. Pritchett eventually would assert of his obliquities, "Faulkner's obscure and rankling genius began to work at the point when, failing to find a place from which to make a judgment, he set to writing about people from the whirlpool inside them, floating along with experience as it came out".) But by that time Faulkner had stopped reading the reviews.

Confident of his own genius, determined to write for himself ("I don't give a damn whether anybody reads my books," he has said) and more perceptive generations to come without reference to current taste, nurturing his private nightmare for purposes which perhaps eluded his own understanding, he had begun to regard critics and the literary world in general with indifference and contempt. When publishers sent books to him, hopeful of a comment which they could use in advertising or on jacket "blurbs," he often tossed them in his wastebasket; by local report they were subsequently, at his order, used by his Negro houseboy to help fill in a ditch on the property. With his withdrawal he became increasingly anti-intellectual, drawing over himself the mantle of the simple, rough "farmer" who "happened to write sometimes." When Ilya Ehrenberg and a group of Soviet writers visited this country on a tour sponsored by the State Department (in the days when this was not only a permissible but a laudable project) and named Faulkner as someone they were most eager to meet, he at first refused entirely. Then, when the Department appealed to his patriotism, he agreed to receive them if they would limit their visit to ten minutes. "Hell," he said, "they'd want to talk about ideas. I'm not interested in ideas. I'm a writer, not a literary man." The Russians were offended at this condition and did not come.

And indeed, during the 1940's, he could characterize himself as a "farmer" with some accuracy. Following *The Hamlet*, published in 1940, there was no new book from him during the whole decade. He was writing short stories during this time, and working intermittently after 1944 on *A Fable* (his newest book, of which more will be said here later), and finally producing *Intruder in the Dust*, so that he was by no means unoccupied with writing. Nevertheless the almost ferocious productivity of the years around 1930 had no later parallel; and in his own analogy about writing—"It's like ridin' a horse. A man may feel like ridin', so he goes out and rides, and then he may not feel like it for awhile. Sometimes I don't feel like writin' and then again I do, and I write a lot"—he did not feel like riding the Pegasus of his peculiar imagination. He did not feel like it—or could not. This relative impotence was perhaps not only an effect but a cause of alcoholic escape. As he indicated, in answering some questions put to him by an English class at Ole Miss, he was consciously aware of a loss of power. "I feel I'm written out," he said. "I don't think I'll write much more. You have only so much steam and if you don't use it up in writing it'll get off by itself."

(In this same classroom interview, in answer to the question as to how he ranked himself among contemporary writers, he answered: "1. Thomas Wolfe: he had much courage and wrote as if he didn't have long to live; 2. William Faulkner; 3. Dos Passos; 4. Ernest Hemingway: he has no courage, has never crawled out on a limb. He has never been known to use a word that might cause the reader to check with a dictionary to see if it is properly used; 5. John Steinbeck: at one time I had great hopes for him—now I don't know.")

In Europe, where his audience had always been friendlier than in the United States—where, in fact, he was widely held to be the greatest American writer of his generation—and especially in France, his prestige remained high. To Gide he was "one of the most important, perhaps *the* most important American writer"; to Claude Magny, "the only modern novelist who had lived, in all its magnitude, the literary drama of the age . . . His work has laid down the prerequisites of Salvation." Malraux, writing the preface to the French edition of *Sanctuary*, declared that in that work "the Greek tragedy has entered the realm of the crime story." Jean Paul Sartre and his followers, identifying his "cosmic pessimism" (a critic's phrase of which Miss Maud had said, "I declare I don't know what that means, and I don't think Billy does either") with their own vision of a cruel and senseless universe, put him officially in the Existentialist pantheon.

In this country, however, by the mid-40's, he had already begun to seem somehow a figure from the past, a major figure to be sure, one whose influence was felt throughout contemporary literature and had inspired a whole school of imitators (the South was now full of young neo-Faulknerians, brooding, tangential, futile, violent, and sad) but whose significance, like Scot Fitzgerald's, was largely historic. He was studied in college writing and literary courses; he was written about in academic journals; but otherwise he was read by very few. All of his books but *Sanctuary* were out of print, and during the war the plates for some had been given to the scrap metal drive.

In 1945 Malcolm Cowley, who previously had edited a successful collection of Hemingway's writing for the Viking Portable Library, became interested in doing a similar volume on Faulkner. He found that the books were unavailable not only at the regular book stores but even at most second-hand stores. Moreover nobody seemed to have a complete set, not even Faulkner himself. But he managed to get one together and did his *Portable Faulkner*, admirably edited and including a sensible preface and helpful explanatory notes. Faulkner gave his cooperation and approved the preface.

It was the first time that a critic possessing both intelligence and a general audience had taken the trouble to appraise Faulkner's work as a whole, and the first time that the public had been offered a safe and pleasant excursion through the labyrinthine jungle of his prose. The book attracted a great deal of attention. Indeed, although literary "revivals" ordinarily are reserved for the honored dead, it probably is not too much to say that Cowley "revived" Faulkner in the general awareness of his own countrymen.

10

THE NOBEL PRIZE

On the morning of November 10, 1950, Faulkner was liming a field adjoining his home when the news came that he had been awarded the Nobel prize. Estelle ran out from the house to tell him. He seemed pleased. At any rate he stopped work long enough for a brief celebration with her and Jill and the colored help; then he went back to his liming. That night he and Estelle held open house, and friends and relatives swarmed in to congratulate him. He received them courteously and even with some evidence of pleasure; yet there was a contemplative look about him, which soon was explained. He had decided not to go to Stockholm to receive the prize. It was not merely that he disliked ceremonials and public appearances, or even (he told a friend) that he thought the Prize had been demeaned because the judges had "passed over Dreiser and Sherwood Anderson to reward a writer like Sinclair Lewis and Old China

Hand Buck"; it was perhaps also, one may surmise, an ultimate gesture of contempt for the official fame that he felt was long overdue, a regurgitation of the resentment he had felt for criticism and neglect. (A very close relative has said, with distress, "Bill can't stand anything except absolute adulation.")

It was Jill who at last changed his mind. Every young girl ought to see Paris, he commented, and he didn't want to deny Jill the trip.

The exact significance of the Nobel Prize was not widely understood in Oxford, but the townspeople nevertheless realized that it was now necessary to reappraise their native son. "I guess," Leo Calloway would muse later, "he's appreciated a whole lot more outside than he is around here"; and T. E. Smith would say, still a bit guardedly, "He's an asset to the community although not everybody realizes it." But Phil "Moon" Mullen, the capable editor of the weekly *Oxford Eagle*, played the event top and center on the front page, adjacent to and as big as the school board's recommendation to the board of aldermen for a $625,000 building program, with a picture of Faulkner, the news story, and reminiscences on Faulkner by Phil Stone, "Mack" Reed, and Ike Roberts. Stone, after telling about Faulkner's career, ended with this tribute: ". . . Bill and I are getting to be old men now and perhaps someone who knows should say it, someone who knows that he is even greater as a man than he is as a writer. A lot of us talk about decency, about honor, about loyalty, about gratitude. Bill doesn't talk about these things; he lives them. Other people may desert you but not Bill, if he is your friend. People may persecute you and revile you but this would only bring Bill quickly to your side if you are his friend. If you are his friend and if the mob should choose to crucify you, Bill would be there without summons. He would carry your cross up the hill for you."

A week after the announcement came, Faulkner took off according to custom for the annual hunt in Sharkey County. There was, if not any diffidence, at least a slight uneasiness among some of his companions, who had never thought of him as being famous and who now looked at him with a new curiosity. Aside from the celebrity, and a good deal more impressive than that, the Prize carried an award of $30,000. "Uncle" Ike Roberts was the first to test the new circumstances. "Bill," he said humorously, "now that you got all that money, I hear your head's so big you're not goin' huntin' with me any more." Faulkner said, "Hell, that's just money. They haven't got any deer meat over there." Around the campfire the first night, Ike teased him again: he asked, "Bill, what would you do if that Swede ambassador come down here and handed you that money right now?" Faulkner, who was washing the dishes and had on an apron made of an old cloth sack, replied, "I'd tell him just to put it on that table over there and grab a dryin' rag and help out." The remark was repeated around the camp for days; the normal relationship was reestablished.

But Faulkner drank more than usual as the hunt went on and before long had passed into an alcoholic state from which, as his companions knew, he might not emerge for many days or even some weeks. "Uncle" Ike took charge of him, feeding him soft boiled eggs, whisky punch, and black coffee. Finally, at the end of the hunt, Faulkner was delivered to his home and relays of friends and relatives began the familiar process—now an extraordinarily tense one—of "setting" with him, hoping the cycle would run its course in time for the scheduled departure for New York and Stockholm, where the award would be made on December 10. As one expedient, the calendar was moved ahead. On Saturday (the next Tuesday on the calendar) as he lay half-conscious in bed, he asked the whereabouts of a male relative and was told he had gone to the high school football game. Faulkner reared up angrily and declared, as it is related: "Somebody's been deceivin' me! They don't play football on Tuesday. I got three more days to drink." At the end of the third day he stopped, and, although pale and shaken, was able to leave with Jill at the appointed time. Stone was among the little group of friends and relatives who saw them off, and cautioned him, "Now Bill, you do right." Faulkner glared and retorted, "I'm so damn sick and tired of hearin' that. Everybody from the Swedish Ambassador to my damn nigger houseboy has been tellin' me to do right." The trip was made without further difficulty.

At the presentation ceremonies in Stockholm Faulkner's distinguished appearance and dignity of manner made an excellent impression. His speech of acknowledgment undoubtedly is one of the great speeches of this century, and already has become a fixture of anthologies. It is given here in full:

"I feel that this award was not made to me as a man but to my work—a life's work in the agony and sweat of the human spirit, not for glory and least of all for profit, but to create out of the materials of the human spirit something which did not exist before. So this award is only mine in trust. It will not be difficult to find a dedication for the money part of it commensurate with the purpose and significance of its origin.* But I would like to do the same with the acclaim too, by using this moment as a pinnacle from which I might be

* According to Judge Faulkner, who handled the legal matters involved, he turned it over to a Faulkner Memorial Fund, with Jill, Mack Reed, cousin J. W. T. IV, and brother John as trustees. He reserved the right to use $5,000 during his own lifetime for good works of his own choosing. The credit balance, with interest, will be available after his death for scholarships and books for deserving Lafayette County students.

listened to by the young men and women already dedicated to the same anguish and travail, among whom is already that one who will some day stand here where I am standing.

"Our tragedy today is a general and universal physical fear so long sustained by now that we can even bear it. There are no longer problems of the spirit. There is only the question: When will I be blown up? Because of this, the young man or woman writing today has forgotten the problems of the human heart in conflict with itself which alone can make good writing because only that is worth writing about, worth the agony and the sweat.

"He must learn them again. He must teach himself that the basest of all things is to be afraid; and, teaching himself that, forget it forever, leaving no room in his workshop for anything but the old verities and truths of the heart, the old universal truths lacking which any story is ephemeral and doomed—love and honor and pity and pride and compassion and sacrifice. Until he does so, he labors under a curse. He writes not of love but of lust, of defeats in which nobody loses anything of value, of victories without hope and, worst of all, without pity or compassion. His griefs grieve on no universal bones, leaving no scars. He writes not of the heart but of the glands.

"Until he relearns these things, he will write as though

he stood among and watched the end of man. I decline to accept the end of man. It is easy enough to say that man is immortal simply because he will endure; that when the last ding-dong of doom has clanged and faded from the last worthless rock hanging tideless in the last red and dying evening, that even then there will still be one more sound: that of his puny inexhaustible voice, still talking. I refuse to accept this. I believe that man will not merely endure: he will prevail. He is immortal, not because he alone among creatures has an inexhaustible voice but because he has a soul, a spirit capable of compassion and sacrifice and endurance. The poet's, the writer's, duty is to write about these things. It is his privilege to help man endure by lifting his heart, by reminding him of the courage and honor and hope and pride and compassion and pity and sacrifice which have been the glory of his past. The poet's voice need not merely be the record of man, it can be one of the props, the pillars to help him endure and prevail."

On his return to Oxford the town wanted to honor him, to do something to show it appreciated the honor that had come to it through him. There was talk of a plaque or a monument. At a chamber of commerce lunch Sykes Haney, the Chevrolet dealer, hit on what at first seemed a happy thought: to change the civic slogan on the water tower from "Oxford, home of Ole Miss" to

"Oxford, home of Ole Miss and William Faulkner." But Bill Griffin, Secretary of the Ole Miss Alumni Association, rose to object that there is a difference, after all, between a great institution and an individual. Finally it was decided to have a fish fry and invite him as the guest of honor. This invitation was forwarded to Faulkner, who very courteously accepted.

11

A FABLE

Writing The Book has been like tryin' to write the Lord's Prayer on the head of a pin. You try to say and sum up something, an impression of life, in what necessarily is a small space, and you're given only sixty years to do it in. Savin' a few exceptions that's all anybody has; a short time.

WILLIAM FAULKNER

William Faulkner, at the time this biography was written, was fifty-seven years old; not old, in the common definition of age, but by his definition nearing the end of creative life and, as he has said, conscious of a diminution in his powers. It would be both rash and presumptuous to make any final summary of his life and works now, for he writes, as he says, "answerin' the call of my own demon," and the results are unforeseeable. Yet, on the evidence of his last books, one is inclined to agree with his belief that his major achievements are behind him: "Any good carpenter knows where the woodpile is and where to get the nails. And finally he knows that this nail ain't as straight or true as the nail he drove a few years ago." The remainder of his creative life may be not so much a continuation as an addendum, a footnote to his genius.

"A life's work spent in the agony and sweat of the human spirit" has brought a sense of failure, he has said. Failure—because he has not succeeded in originating a true and great American kind of writing, as he believes Hemingway also has failed, and even Sherwood Anderson. Thomas Wolfe might have done it, he believes, if he had lived long enough.

Failing of this "grand design," he has, however, in his own phrase, achieved through the Nobel Prize "a scratch on the face of anonymity." And by the peculiar ambivalence of his character, this has had some noteworthy effects.

Following the Nobel Prize, his public character has undergone modifications which a few years previously would have seemed impossible. He has appeared on television—on a culturally ambitious program called "Omnibus." He has even made public speeches: not, to be sure, before the chamber of commerce (which asked him) but before the Farm Bureau, of which he approves, and before the high school and junior college graduating classes of his daughter. The high school speech, following closely on and echoing in part the Nobel Prize speech, is especially worth recording:

". . . It is not men in the mass who can and will save Man. It is Man himself, created in the image of God so that he shall have the power and the will to choose right from wrong, and so be able to save himself because he is worth saving—Man, the individual, men and women, who will refuse always to be tricked or frightened or bribed into surrendering, not just the right but the duty too, to choose between justice and injustice, courage and cowardice, sacrifice and greed, pity and self;—who will believe always not only in the right of man to be free of injustice and rapacity and deception, but the duty and responsibility of man to see that justice and truth and pity and compassion are done.

"So, never be afraid. Never be afraid to raise your voice for honesty and truth and compassion, against injustice and lying and greed . . ."

Even less to be expected than Faulkner's late acceptance of himself as a public figure has been his belief that he can no longer write in Oxford. While Jill, following her graduation in 1953 from Pine Manor Junior College, (and before her recent marriage) attended the University of Mexico, and Estelle lived in Mexico City a good part of the year to be near her, Faulkner spent most of his time in New York City. There, in the early winter of 1953, writing at his publisher's office, he finished *A Fable*, thereafter joining Howard Hawks in Europe to write the script of a movie.

A Fable has had an extraordinarily deep and personal meaning for Faulkner. He had great difficulty in writing it. He started it in December, 1944, and worked on it intermittently during the next nine years, putting it aside often, and more than once abandoning it in despair that he would ever be able to finish it. *Intruder in the Dust* and *Requiem for a Nun* (which are not among his best books) were in a sense by-products of his frustration, written in these intervals, with less than his full attention, while the albatross of the unfinished and more important work remained in the background. He took it to Hollywood with him, precipitating a comedy typical of that city: Jack Warner, hearing that he was writing a book "on Warner Brothers' time," declared that it was therefore Warner Brothers' property, and Faulkner's agent had to fend off the claim. Faulkner, with his usual reserve, confided the story to no one except to indicate that it had something to do with the Crucifixion, but in moments of alcoholic exhilaration would speak of it excitedly as the greatest book he had ever done, the pinnacle and summation of his whole career.

In 1951 he published a long fragment of it, almost a novelette, called *Notes on a Horsethief*, about an English groom and an old Negro who steal a crippled race horse, nurse him until he can run again (on three legs) and race him in small towns in the Mississippi Valley until at last the owner's agents find them; whereupon the groom kills the horse to prevent his being retired to stud: ". . . they would have taken it back to the Kentucky farm and shut it up in a whorehouse where it wouldn't need any legs at all . . . because any man can be a father, but only the best, the brave—." The relationship of this Yoknapatawpha-like tale to the purpose of the book remained unknown, however, and caused much speculation among Faulkner's admirers. Rumors gathered as the months and years went on; few books if any have been so talked about before publication, or awaited with such curiosity by critics and the whole world of publishing.

The story that *A Fable* tells is complex even in outline. During the First World War a French corporal —native of an unnamed Middle Eastern country by birth but French by adoption—first converts his twelve-man squad to pacifism and then, with their aid, spreads the message of peace along a large sector of the Western Front. As a result, one day in 1917, a French regiment refuses the order to attack. The regiment is arrested for mutiny and hauled to imprisonment back of the lines. It develops that the Corporal's teachings have permeated the entire front, German as well as Allied: the opposing generals declare a recess of three days until the armies can be brought under control and the fighting resumed. The seriousness of the situation brings to the scene the Allied commander-in-chief, a Marshal of France. The Marshal, it is clear, is to be Pontius Pilate to the Corporal's Christ. As Faulkner manages events, he is to be much more besides.

In his youth, the Marshal had wandered into a mountain valley somewhere in the Middle East and fallen in love there with a woman who was married and had two daughters. She became pregnant by him. He moved on, leaving a purse to buy the unborn child a farm if it was a boy, a dowry if it was a girl. When her time drew near the woman took her two daughters and found refuge in a manger, and on Christmas Eve gave birth to a boy. Dying in childbirth, she gave the purse and the secret of the child's paternity to Marthe ("Magda" in her own country), the nine-year-old daughter (Marya, the eleven-year-old, was feeble-minded). Marthe, resolving to find the baby's father, made herself head of the family and after many wanderings, during which she grew up and married, brought them to France, where she and they settled with her husband on a little farm. There the boy grew up, answered the call when the war came, became a Corporal, and began the activities which led to the mutiny. This part is revealed only very gradually, in flashbacks.

Now—at the beginning of the book—he is to be tried by his father, the Marshal. Marthe comes to plead for his life. She had already realized that the Marshal was the man she had started out, as a child, to seek, for his name was known all over France, but she had put aside the idea in adulthood. Now she brings a locket which he will recognize and which will convince him of his paternity. The Marshal recognizes her at once. He needs no convincing. Indeed, it seems that he has already realized that the Corporal is his son. She pleads for the Corporal's life, sensing that the Marshal must refuse, as he does with these words:

". . . if he accept his life, keeps his life, he will have abrogated his own gesture and martyrdom. If I gave him his life tonight, I myself could render null and void what you call the hope and dream of his sacrifice. By destroying his life tomorrow morning, I will establish forever that he didn't even live in vain, let alone die in vain."

But the Marshal, a quasi-God the Father, must also play the part of a quasi-Satan. He takes the Corporal to a mountain top where at first he urges him to escape; then, when the Corporal refuses, offers him the world if he will recant his beliefs. He will acknowledge him as his son (the Corporal somehow has already realized that he is his father) and give him his great name and fortune. But the Corporal refuses, as the Marshal knows he must do, for "we are two articulations [the Marshal says] . . . postulated, not so much to defend as to test two inimical conditions . . . I champion of this mundane earth . . . you champion of an esoteric realm of man's baseless hopes and infinite capacity—no: passion—for unfact." He adds enticingly, if the Corporal should accept his offer, "You will be God, holding him [man] forever through a far, far stronger ingredient than his simple lusts and appetites: by his triumphant and ineradicable folly, his deathless passion for being led, mystified, and deceived."

The parable is played out in detail: the betrayal by Judas (a squad member named Polchek), the denial by Peter (Piotr, another member of the squad), even the strand of barbed wire that curls around the Corporal's head as he falls dead at the hands of a firing squad, flanked by two thieves executed at the same time.

After the war, another squad is sent from Paris to bring back one of the unidentified bodies which had been collected in a fortress near Verdun. They are bribed with 100 francs by a mother who believes the body they take is that of her own dead soldier-son, and end up with the body of the Corporal. They take him back to Paris in a boxcar draped with mourning. The Corporal becomes France's Unknown Soldier.

The heavy burden of symbolism of *A Fable* doubtless will keep Faulkner scholars busy for many years to come. As for its success as a work of art, there will be as many opinions as there are about *Absalom, Absalom!* —the novel that most nearly approximates it in length, complexity, and range of characters and ideas. In it, Faulkner rings the changes with every fault that has been assigned to him in the past, and adds a few new ones. The first two-thirds of the book consists of long fragments only dimly related to one another or to the main story—among them, nearly intact and joined to the narrative only by the flimsiest *rationale*, is *Notes On a Horsethief*, which turns out to have almost nothing to do with events following. The book is laced with long, obscure soliloquies of the most improbable nature, filled with rhetoric so grandiloquent as to be absurd when it is not merely tedious. Nothing is revealed directly if it can be done by reflection; episodes and conversations begin without prior reference to known events or thoughts; nothing is said clearly if it can be obfuscated; characters appear from nowhere and disappear to nowhere; motivations and character development are inexplicable. The book, on the whole, seems demented.

Yet, when one toilsomely and with exasperation and fatigue has plowed through page on page, scene on scene, riddle on riddle and emerged at the final clouded episode (introducing still another new character of whom nothing is known), it is with the emotional depletion of having witnessed, and somehow been deeply and personally if irrationally involved in, a great and infinitely tragic event.

The book was awaited by many of Faulkner's admirers as a revelation of his philosophy, a full and intelligible definition of the obscure Faulknerian contest between good and evil, the nature of which had been hinted at in many of his previous books. Perhaps in the maze of words such a definition is hidden. But, in instances where Faulkner seems to be using characters to convey a universal message, the message is not fresh, only perhaps a little more explicit than before. His triumphant villains (Jason Compson, Flem Snopes, and the others) suspend triumphant but ultimately doomed from this thought, uttered by the wise Marshal:

"Rapacity must not fail, else man must deny he breathes. Not rapacity; its whole vast glorious history repudiates that. It does not, cannot, must not fail . . . Not rapacity, which, like poverty, takes care of its own. Because it endures, not even because it is rapacity but because man is man, enduring and immortal; enduring not because he is immortal but immortal because he endures: and so with rapacity, which immortal man never fails since it is in and from rapacity that he gets, holds, his immortality." And again, some pages later: ". . . people, men and women, don't choose evil and accept it and enter it, but evil chooses the men and women by test and trial, proves and tests them and then accepts them forever until the time comes when they are consumed and empty and at last fail evil because they no longer have anything that evil can want or use; then it destroys them."

The supreme virtue of life, which is to endure (as the admirable Dilsey, the maid in *The Sound and the Fury* endures: as Lena Grove in *Light In August* and various other characters whom Faulkner seems to admire also endure), is enunciated again by the old Marshal in an interchange on the mountain top with the Corporal:

"Oh yes, he (man) will survive . . . because he has that in him which will endure even beyond the ultimate worthless tideless rock freezing slowly in the last red and heatless sunset, because already the next star in the blue immensity of space will be already clamorous with the uproar of his debarkation, his puny and inexhaustible voice still talking, still planning; and there too after the last ding dong of doom has rung and died there will still be one sound more: his voice, planning still to build something higher and faster and louder; more efficient and louder and faster than ever before, yet it too inherent with the same old primordial fault since it too in the end will fail to eradicate him from the earth. I don't fear man. I do better: I respect and admire him. And pride: I am ten times prouder of that immortality which he does possess than ever he of that heavenly one of his delusion. Because man and his folly—"

"Will endure," the Corporal said.

"They will do more," the old General said proudly. "They will prevail . . ."

This, then, evidently is the supreme insight of a "life's work spent in the agony and sweat of the human spirit": a belief in man's endurance, in his ability to prevail—by mere endurance, and by "pity and pride and compassion and sacrifice"—over the evil that bestrides the world: that is the world.

How to sum up Faulkner? In one of Conrad Aiken's essays he introduces in that connection a quotation from Henry James:

"He is at once one of the most corrupt of writers and one of the most naïf, the most mechanical and pedantic, and the fullest of *bonhomie* and natural impulse. He is one of the finest of artists and one of the coarsest. Viewed in one way, his novels are ponderous, shapeless, overloaded; his touch is graceless, violent, barbarous. Viewed in another, his tales have more color, more composition, more grasp of the reader's attention than any others. [His] style would demand a chapter apart. It is the least simple style, probably, that ever was written; it bristles, it cracks, it swells and swaggers; but it is a perfect expression of the man's genius. Like his genius, it contains a certain quantity of everything, from immaculate gold to flagrant dross. He was a very bad writer, and yet unquestionably he was a very great writer. We may say briefly, that in so far as his method was an instinct it was successful, and that in so far as it was a theory it was a failure. But both in instinct and in theory he had the aid of an immense force of conviction. His imagination warmed to his work so intensely that there was nothing his volition could not impose upon it. Hallucination settled upon him, and he believed anything that was necessary in the circumstances."

But James, of course, was not writing about Faulkner. He was writing about Balzac.

Set in Linotype Scotch
Format by Robert Cheney
Manufactured by The Haddon Craftsmen, Inc.
Published by HARPER & BROTHERS, *New York*